NO LON~~~~~ ~~~~~~F
SEATT~~~~~~~~~~~~~ ~~Y

D0399038

Thoughts of Dog

hello.
it's me again.
i love you

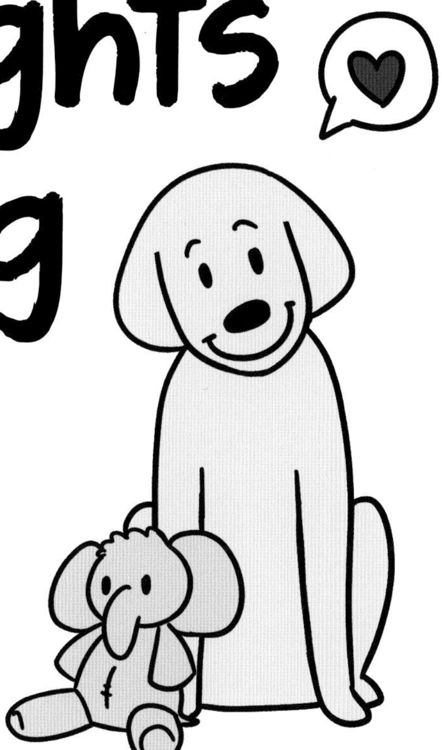

Thoughts of Dog

Matt Nelson

aka @dog_feelings

Andrews McMeel

PUBLISHING®

Winter

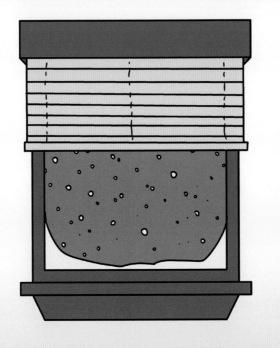

snow is just fancy rain. taking its time. i like to think
i am just as fancy. when my paws are crossed

i was only outside for a minute. when a snowflake landed on my nose.

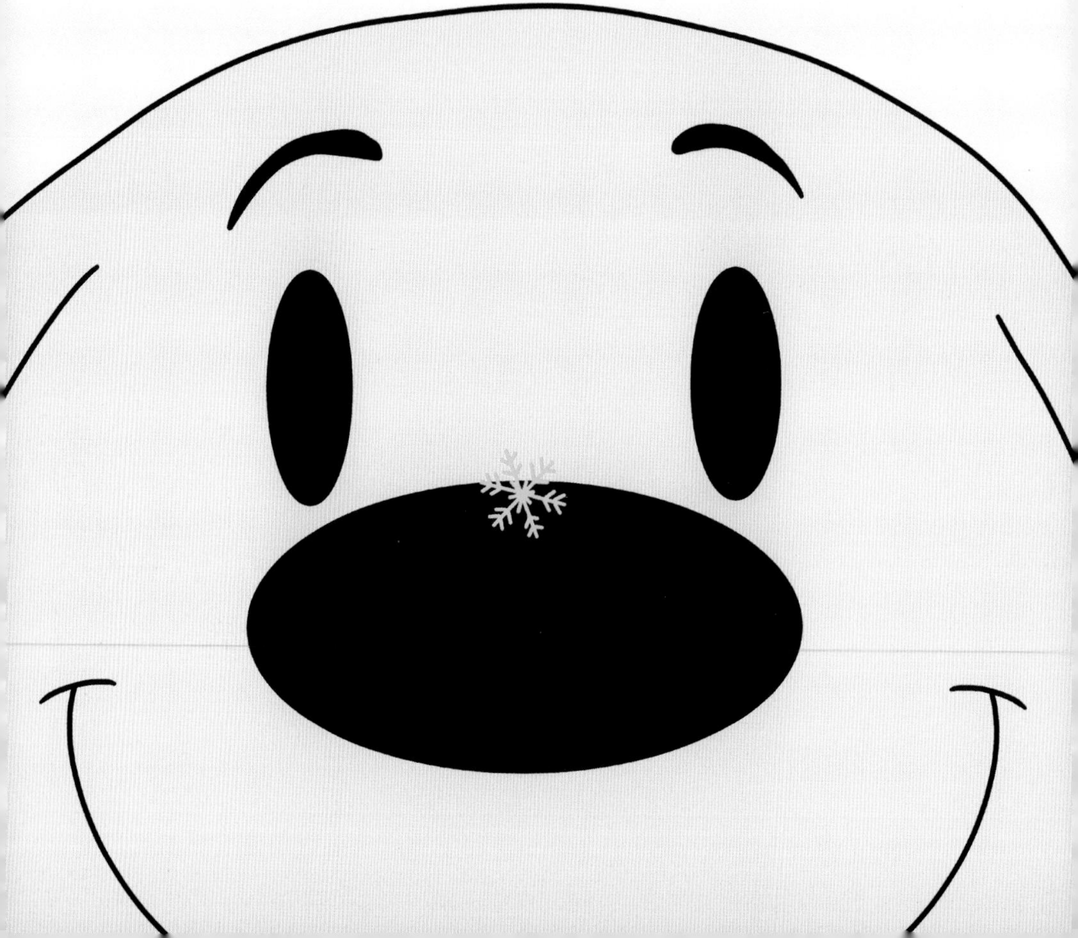

i hurried inside. to show my stuffed fren sebastian. but by the time i got to him. my wintry pal was gone

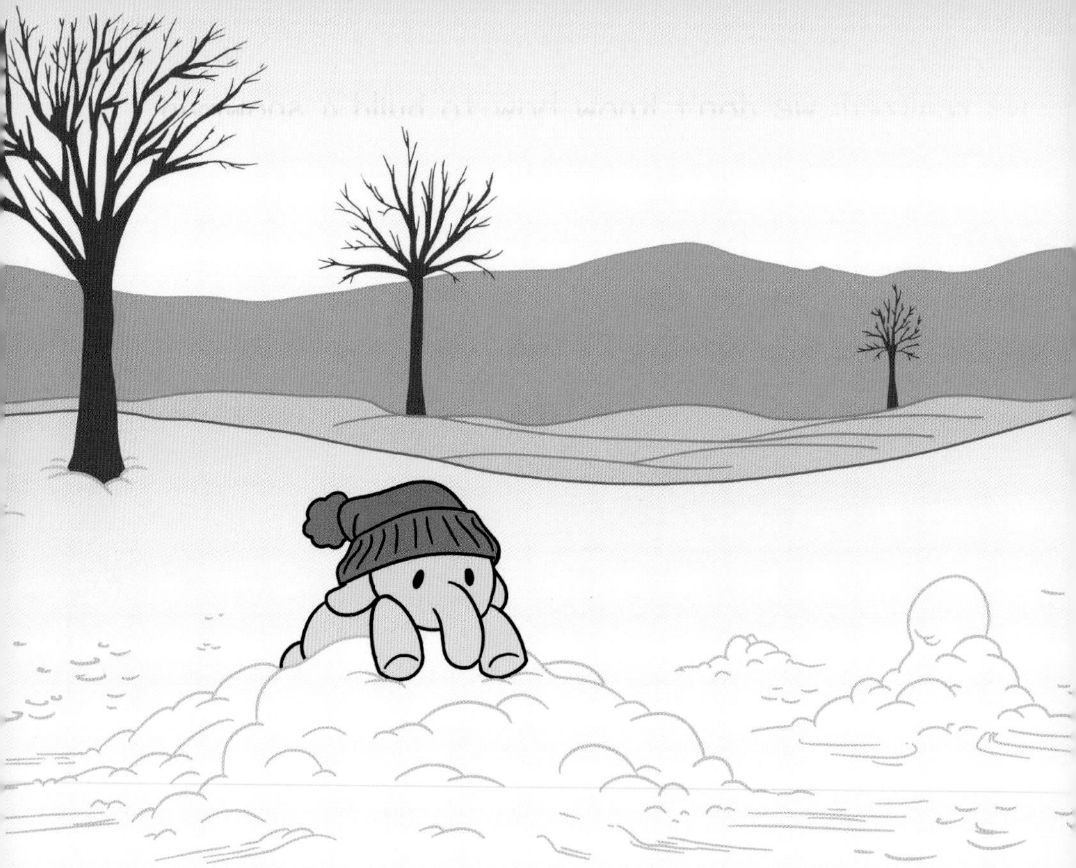

my stuffed fren sebastian and i. have decided to build a snowman.

but after several minutes of staring at each other.
we realized. we don't know how to build a snowman

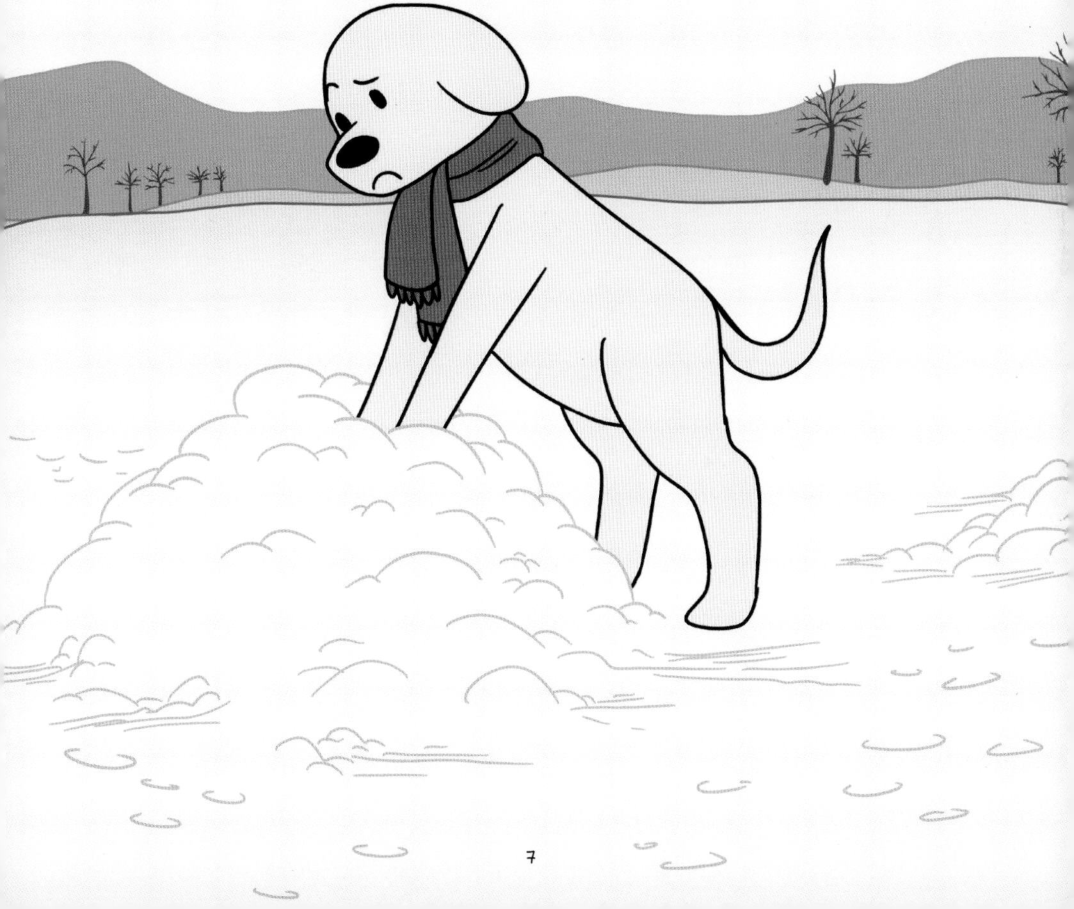

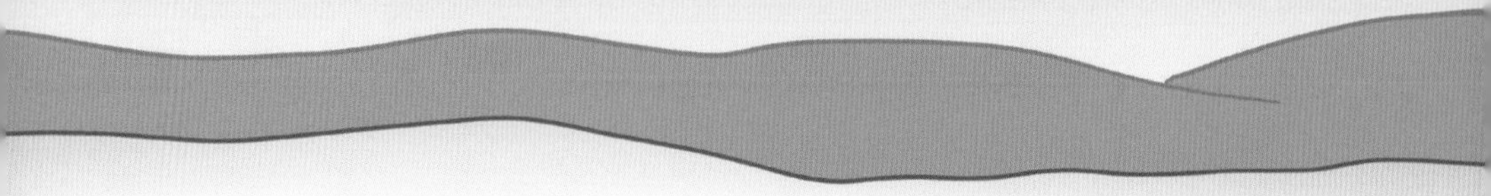

we have joined forces with the human. to build the snowman. apparently it requires a very specific skillset. and opposable thumbs. but do not worry. we helped as much as we could

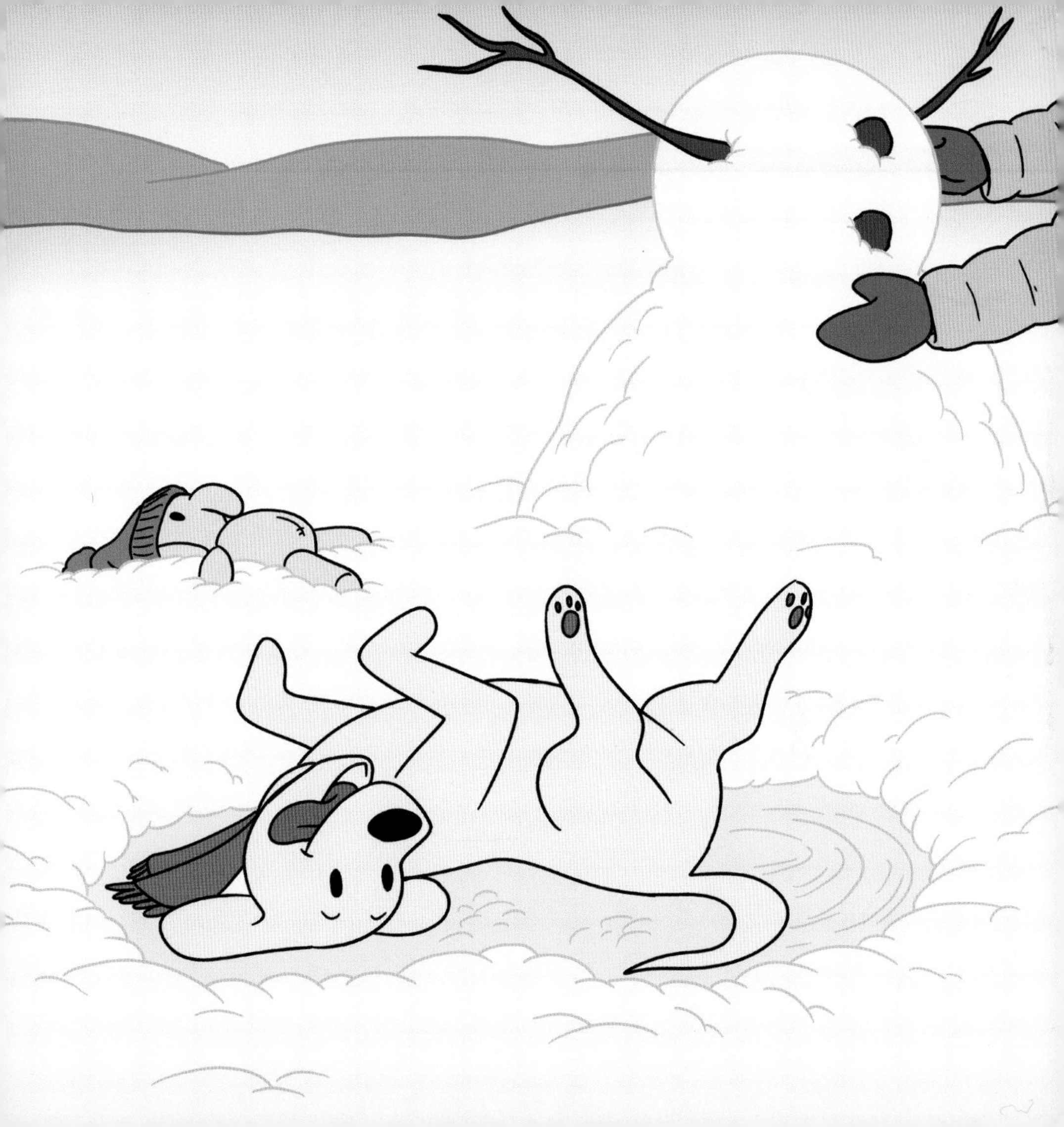

as the human put the final touches on the snowman. they were also kind enough to bring me a snack. today was a pretty good day

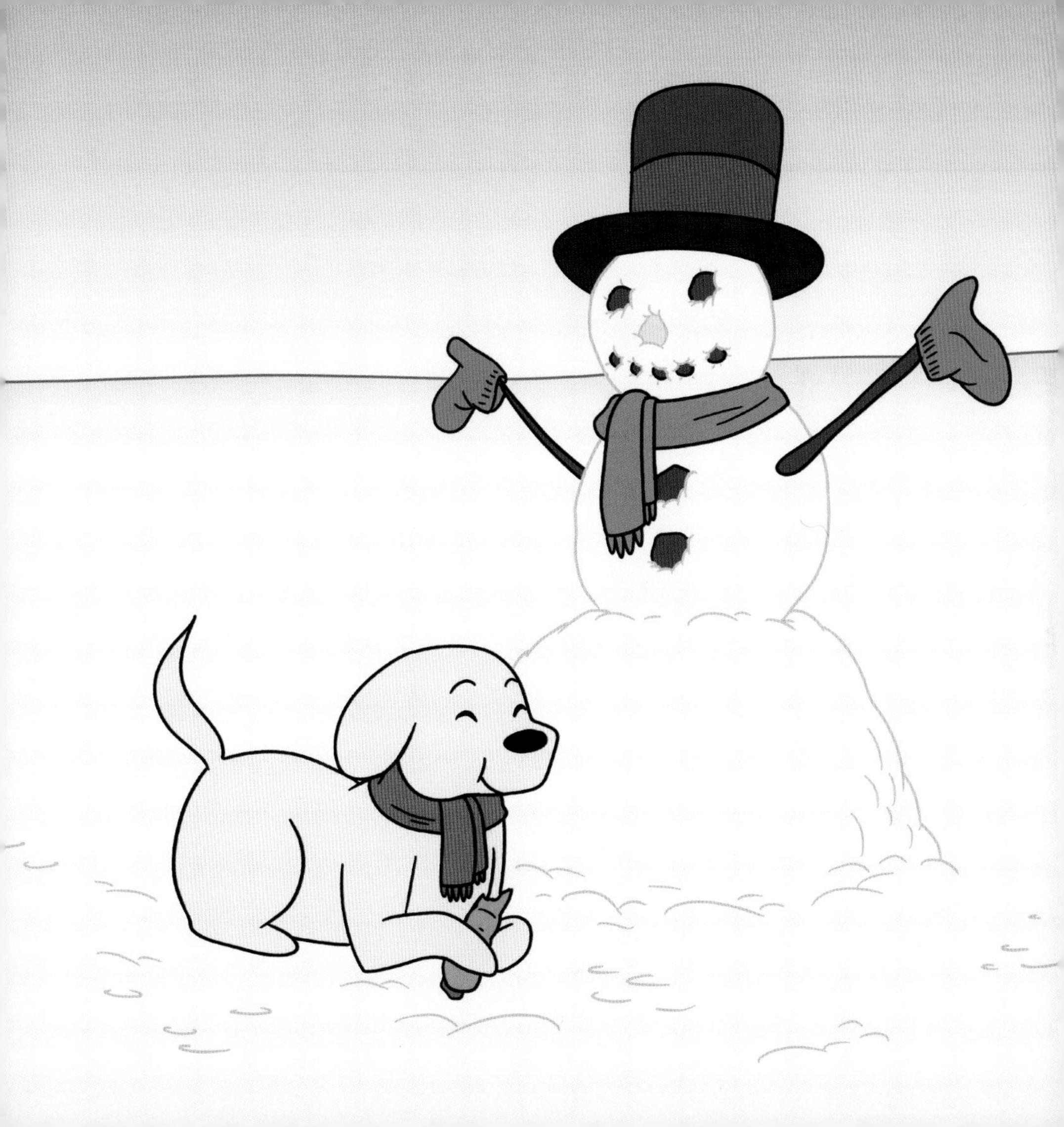

Movie Night

the human is hosting a movie night. and i am supposed
to greet all the guests. without jumping on them.
a nearly impossible task

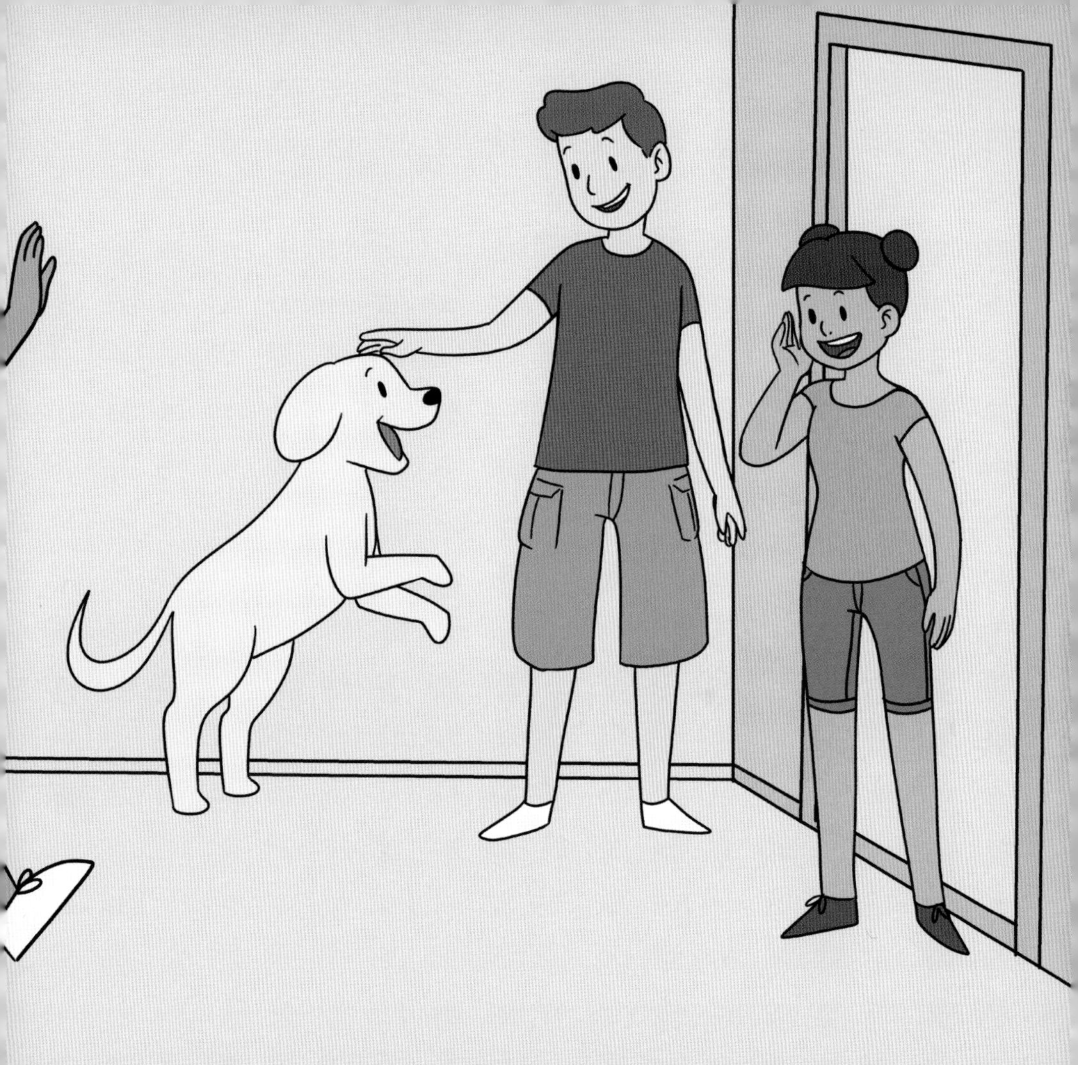

i am cuddling with my stuffed fren sebastian. the human is cuddling with me. and the human is also cuddling with their fren.

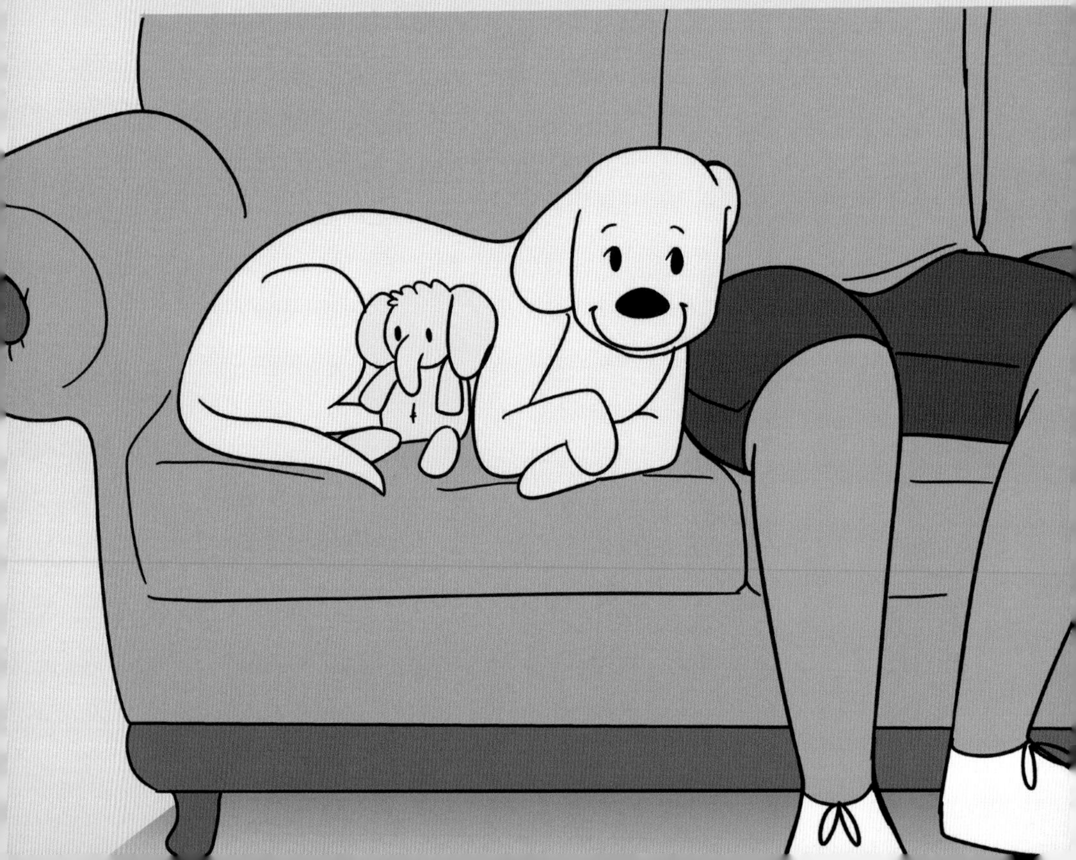

according to the transitive property of cuddles.
the human's fren is also cuddling sebastian

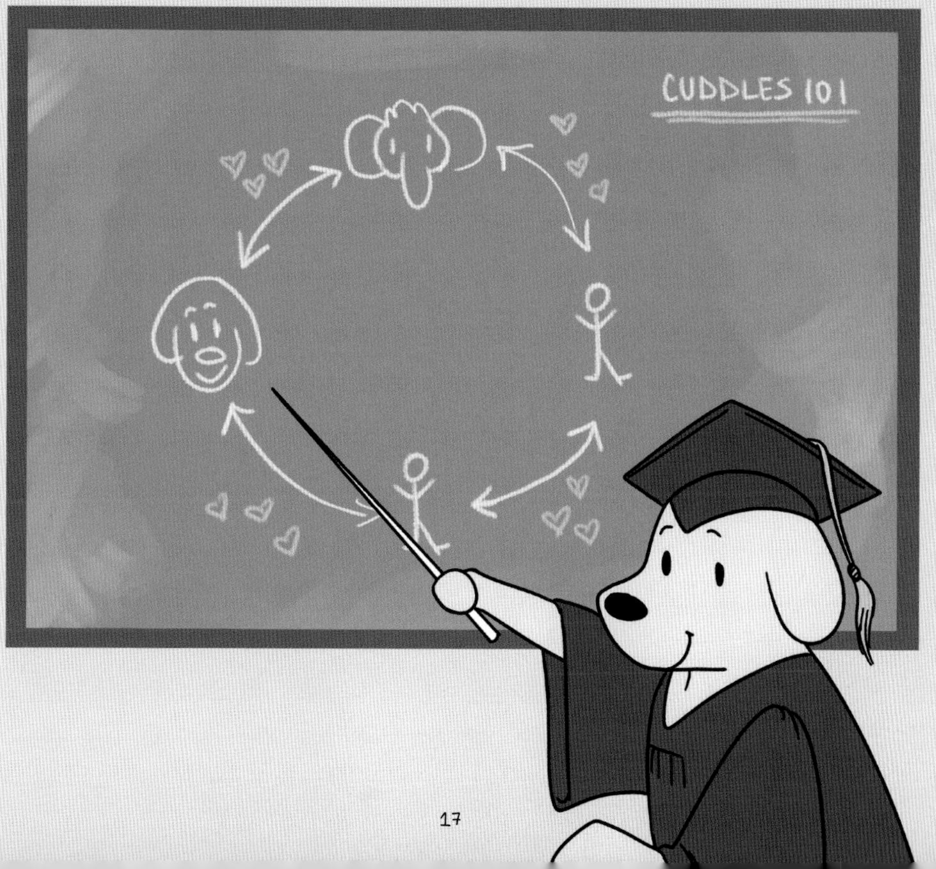
CUDDLES 101

i decided it was selfish. to keep sebastian to myself during the movie. so i passed him around. and let everyone get their share of cuddles

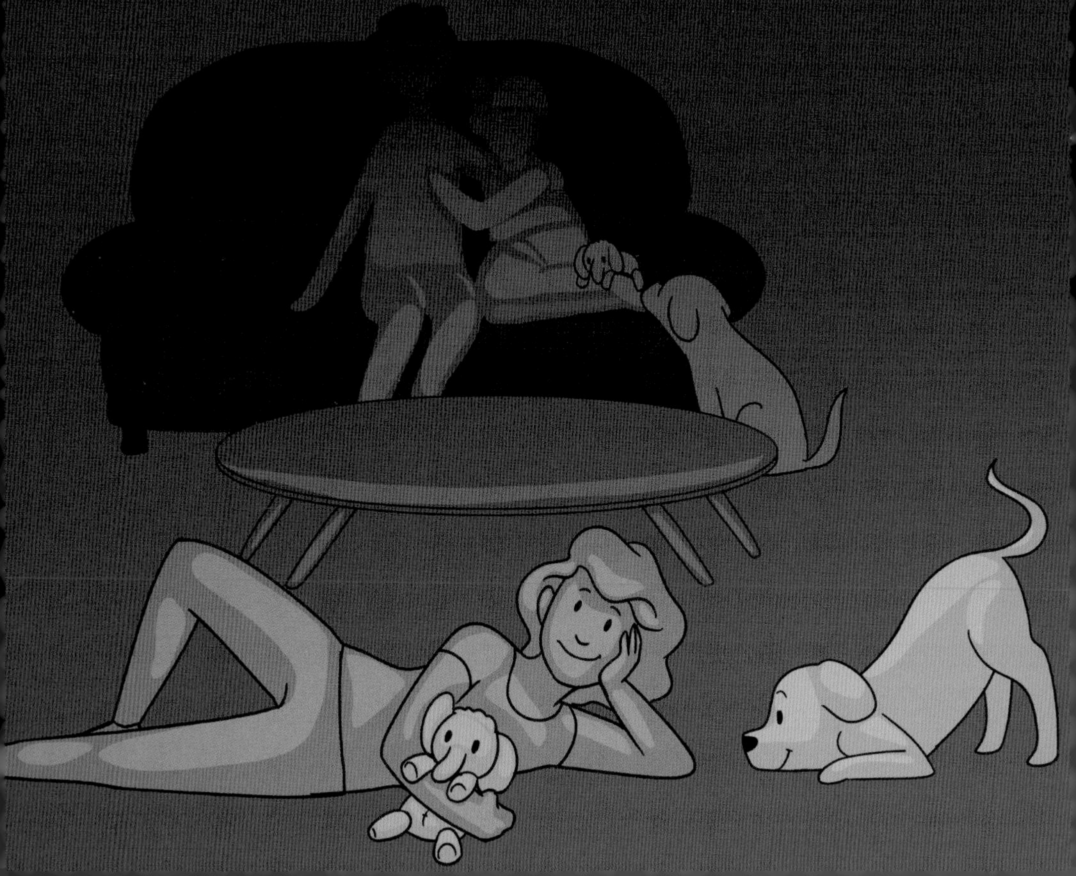

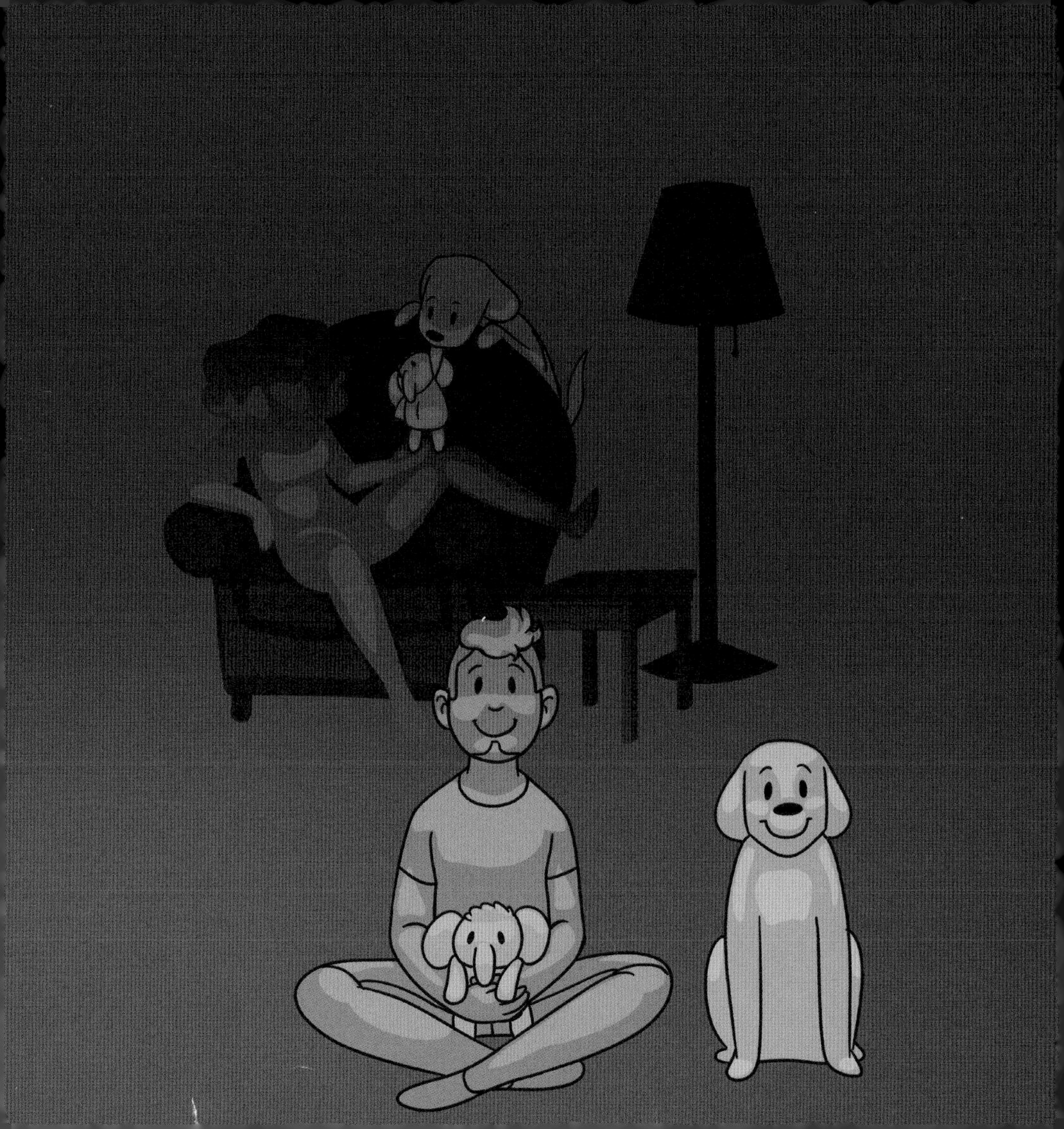

one of the human's frens. cuddled with my stuffed fren sebastian for quite a while. eventually i had to go confiscate him. because no matter what. i get to cuddle with him the most

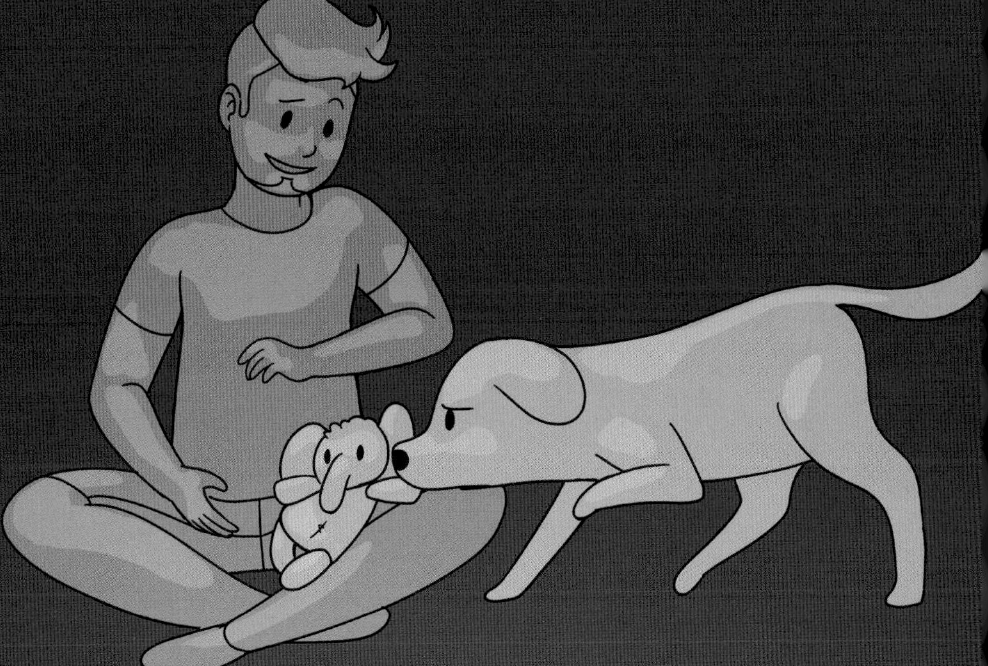

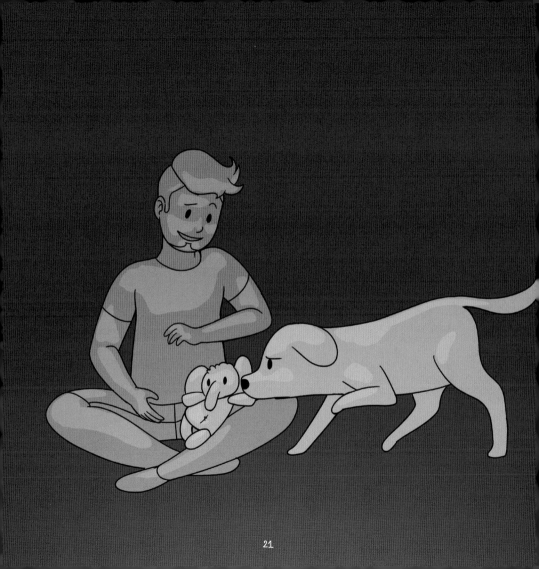

i always really enjoy movie nights. but the human gets a little annoyed with me. apparently i fall asleep during all the good parts. which i would argue. doesn't support the argument. that they're the good parts

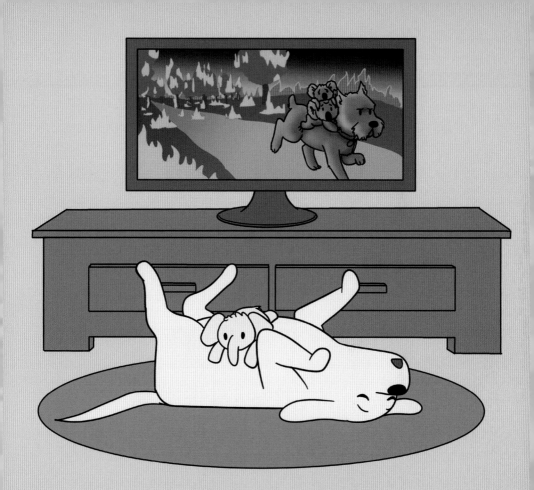

Sebastian Goes to Work

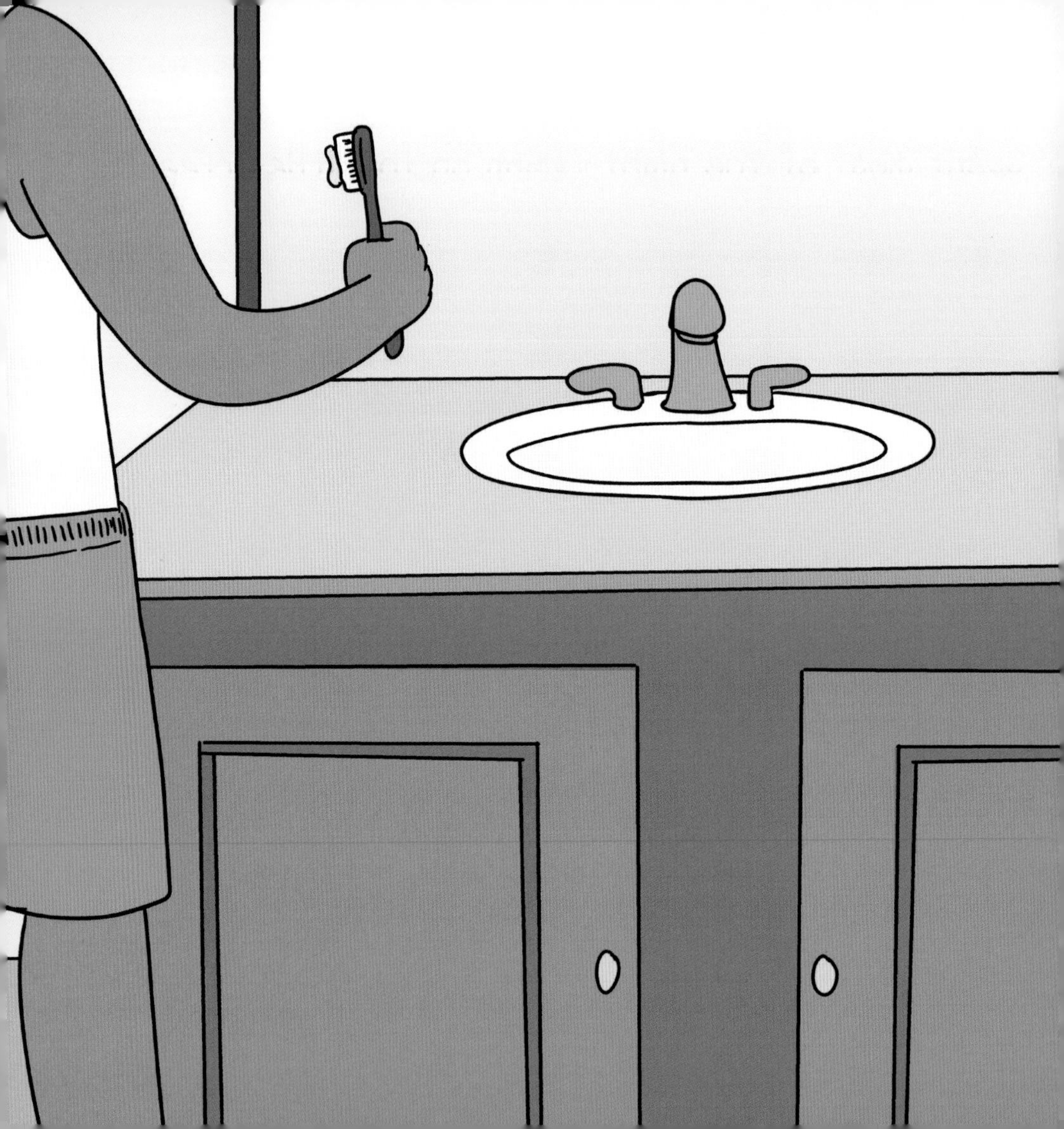

the human seems extra stressed this morning. they spent most of the night typing on the little screen. barely dreaming at all.

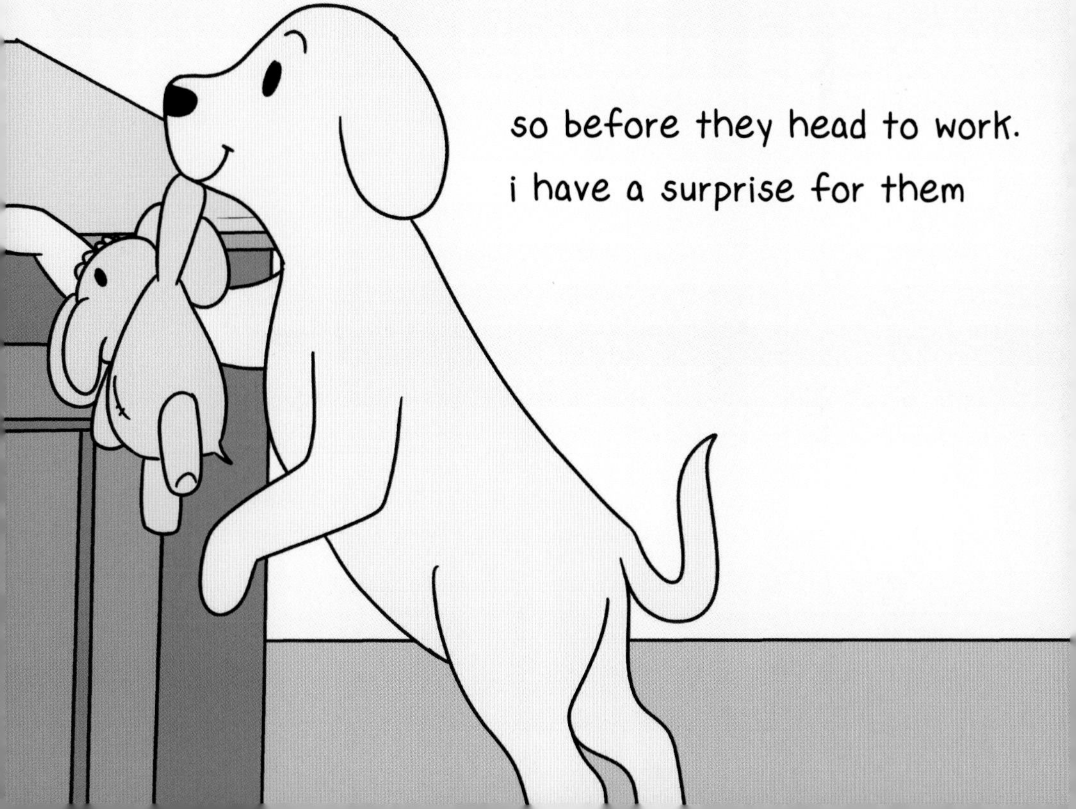

so before they head to work. i have a surprise for them

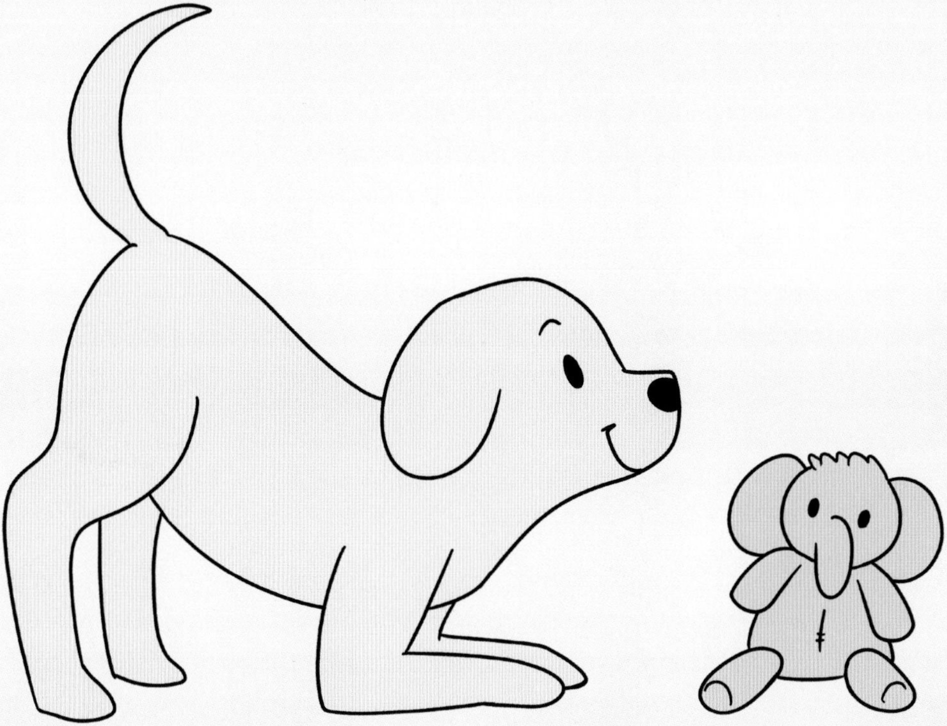

it's my stuffed fren sebastian. i'm letting the human take him today.

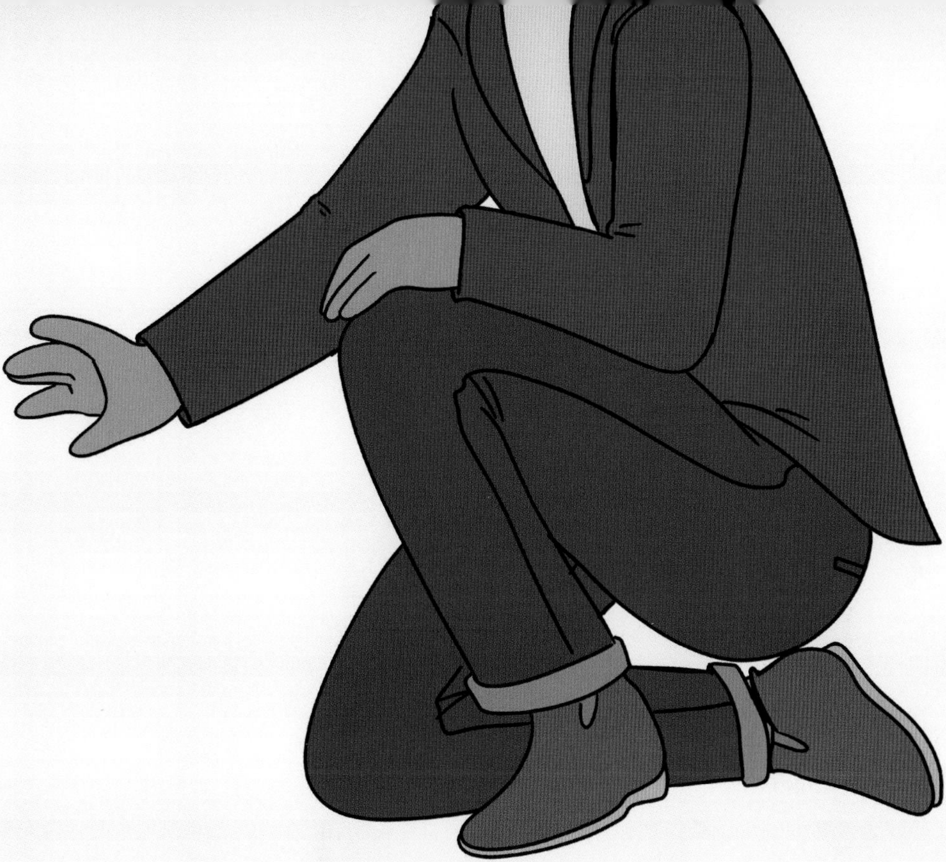

this is an incredibly enticing offer. i would be very surprised if the human turned it down

my stuffed fren sebastian. is on his way to work with the human. they were reluctant at first. but when i insisted. they took him by the hoof. placed him in their backpack. and were on their way

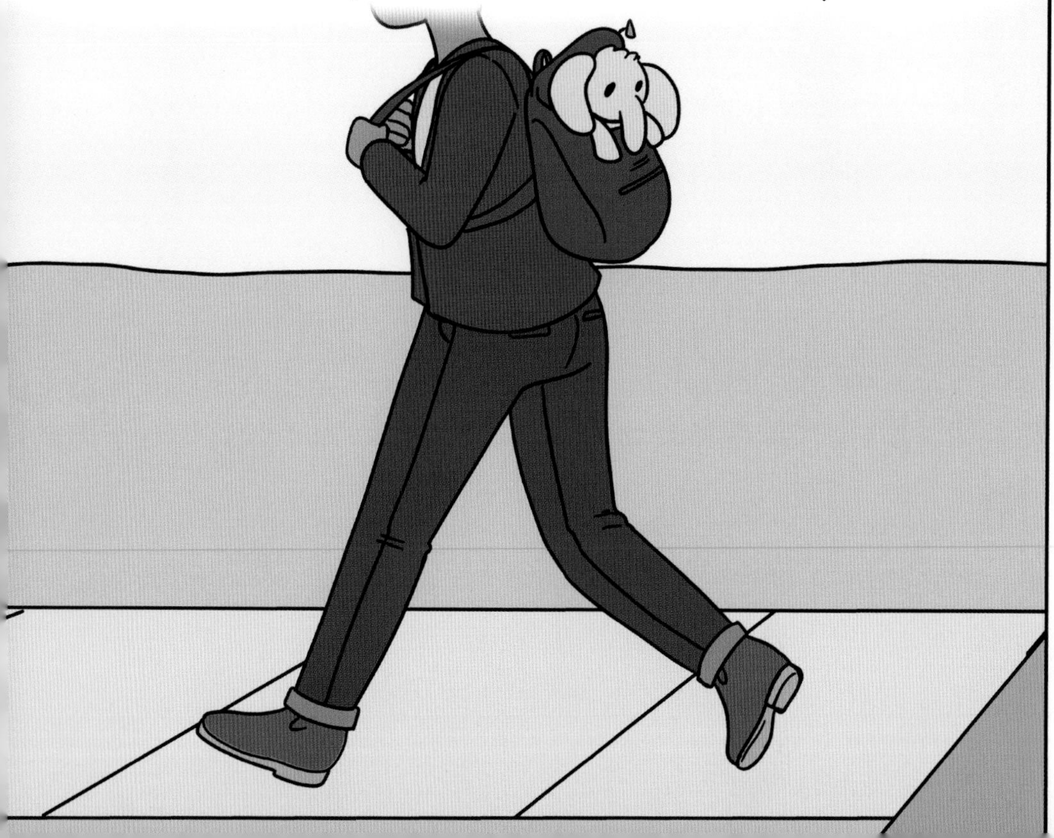

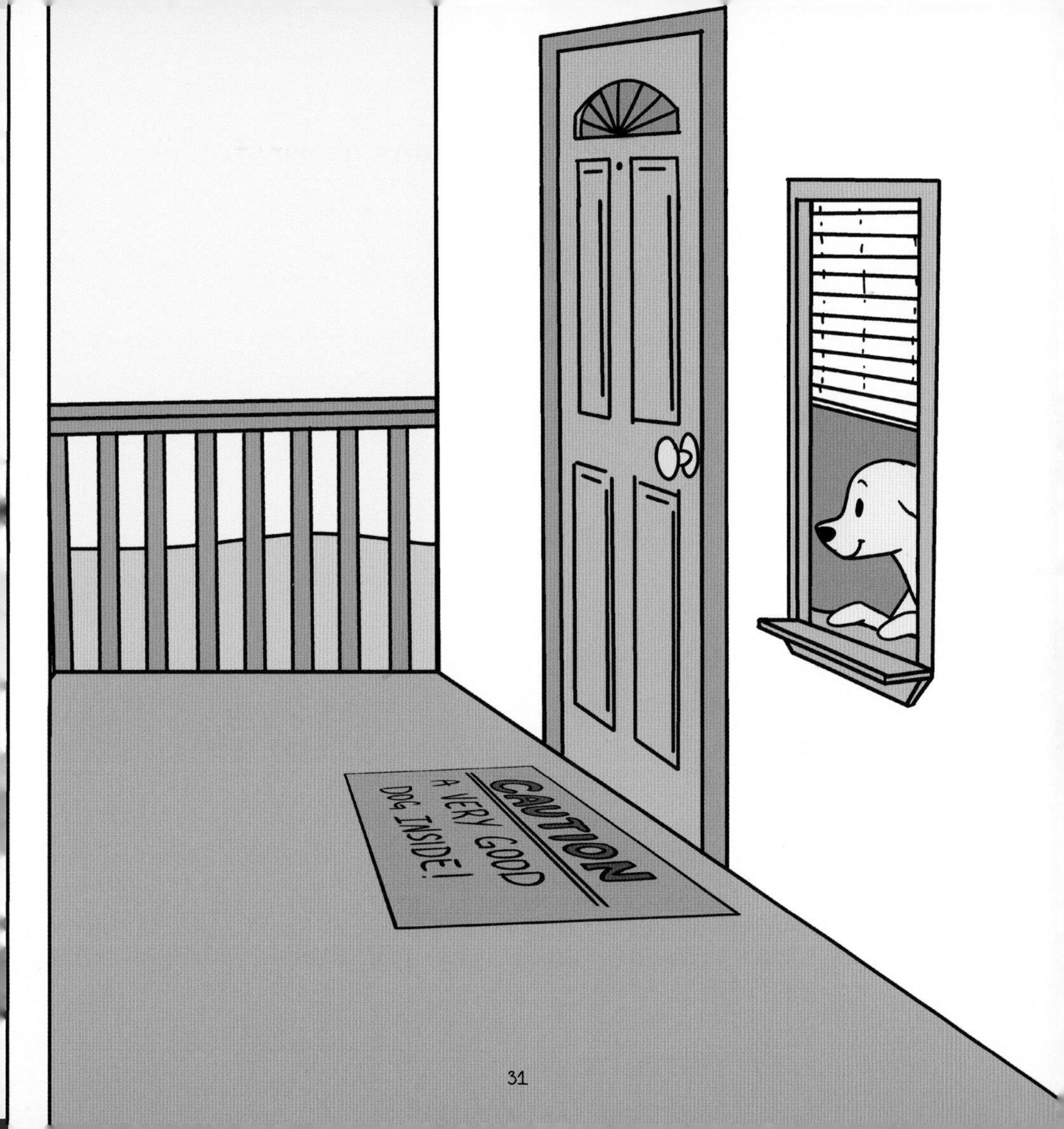
CAUTION
A VERY GOOD
DOG INSIDE!

i've been alone in the household for a bit now. and when i get a little lonely. i just imagine the human explaining to the other humans. why they have a stuffed elephant at work

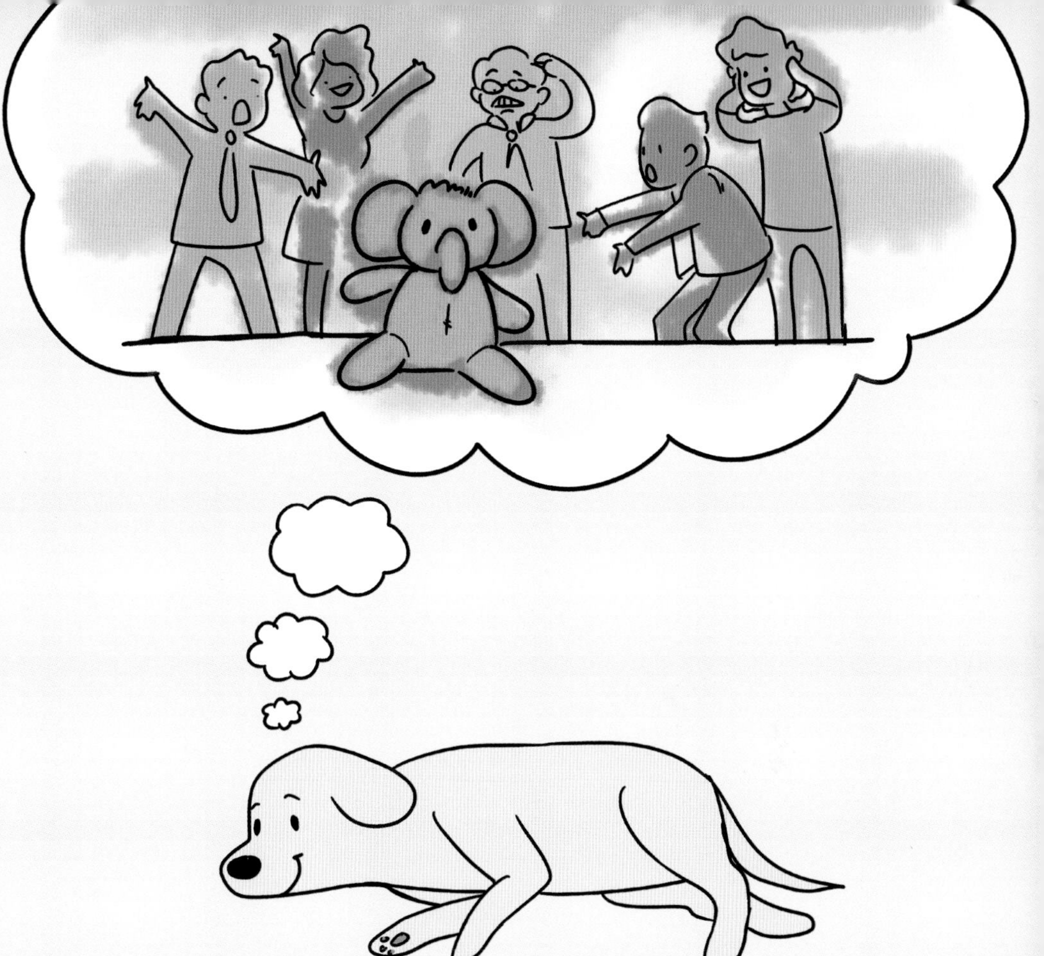

usually between my midafternoon snoozle. and my late midafternoon snoozle. i will wiggle on my back a bit. sebastian likes to watch this. but today i didn't have an audience. and it just wasn't the same

THE GARAGE DOOR IS OPENING. THE HUMAN AND SEBASTIAN HAVE RETURNED. EVERYTHING IS LOVELY. MY FEETS ARE A TIPPY TAPPIN

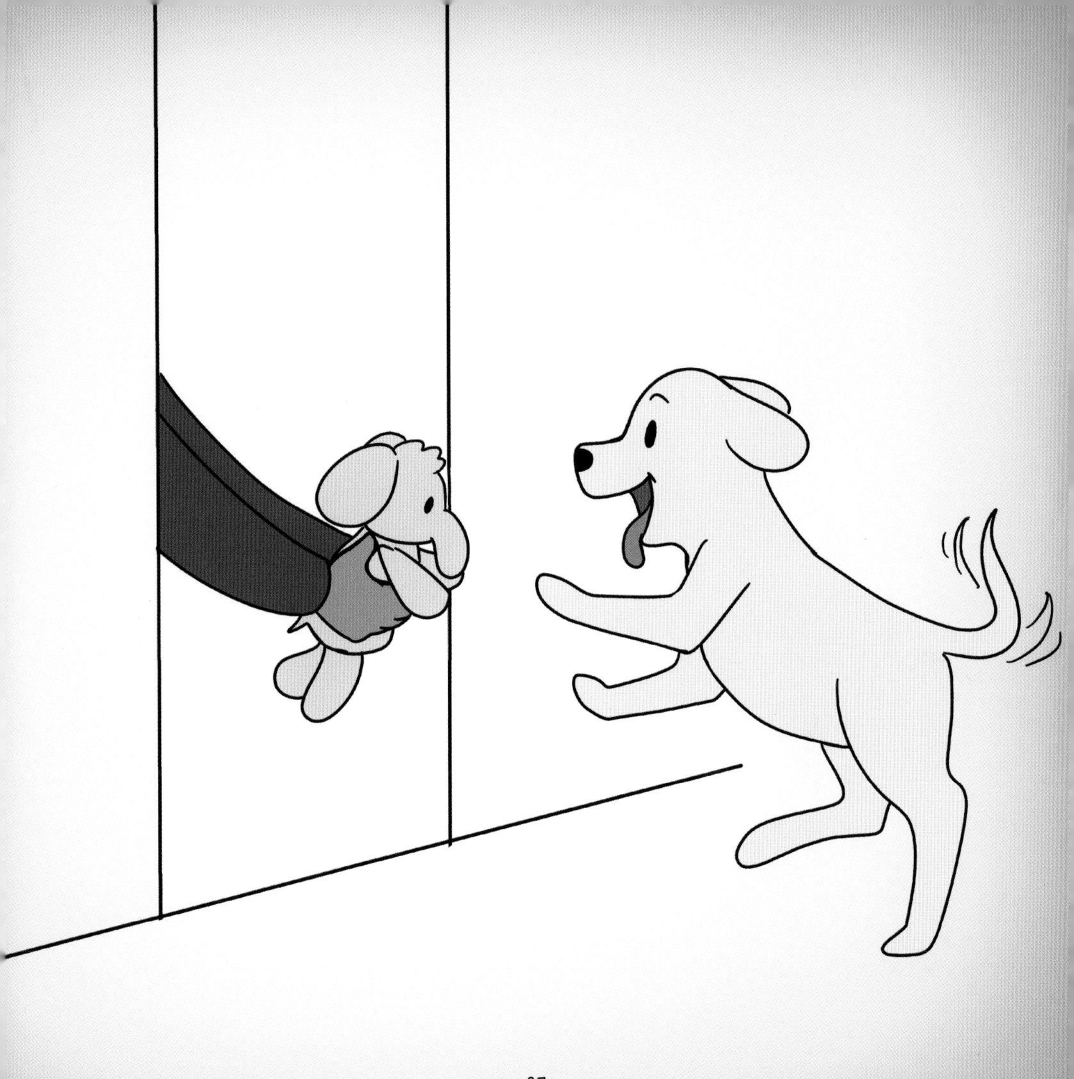

Beach

the human was more excited than usual. when they got
home from work today. apparently they have decided.
we are taking an overdue vacation. to the big water

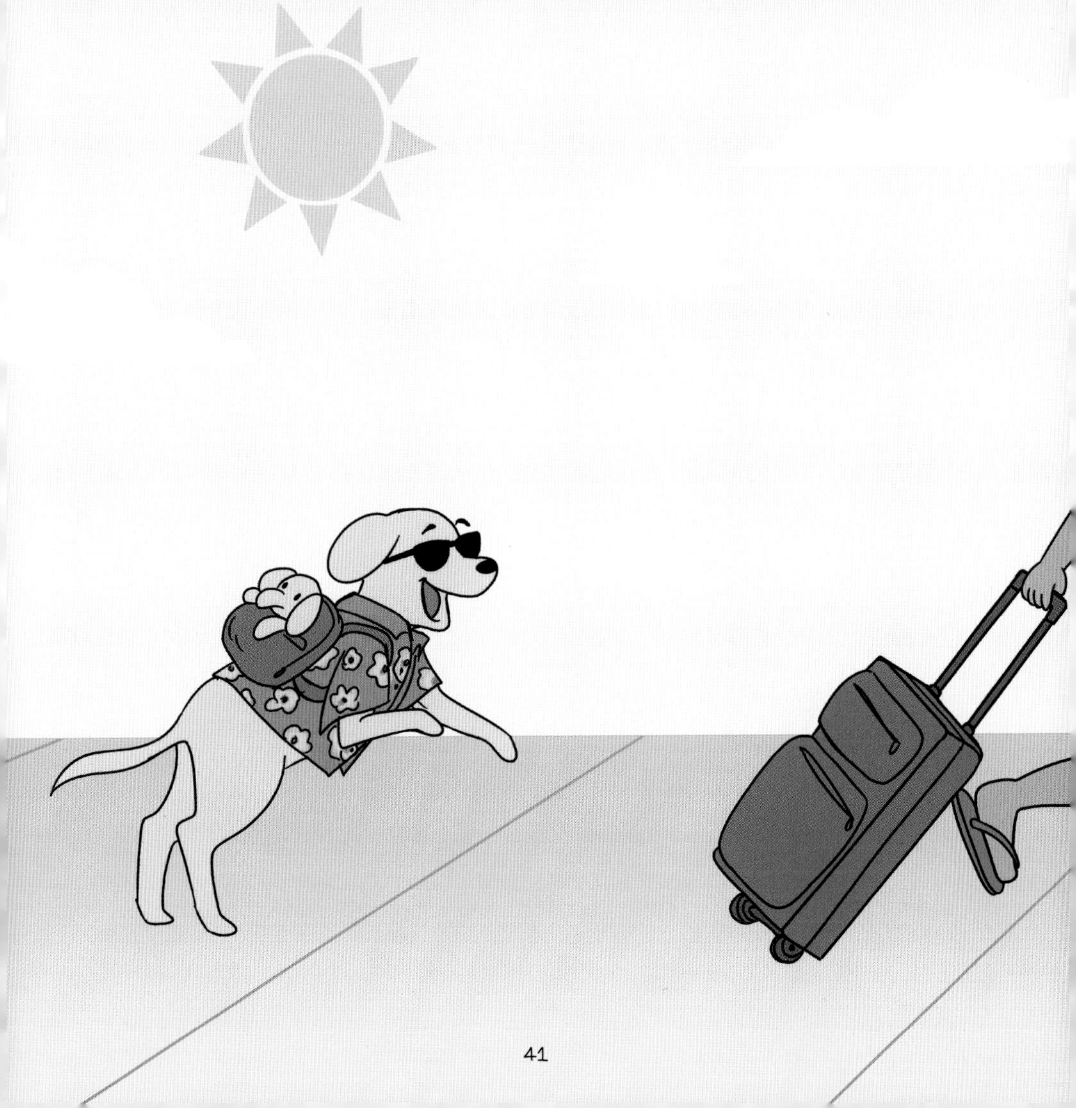

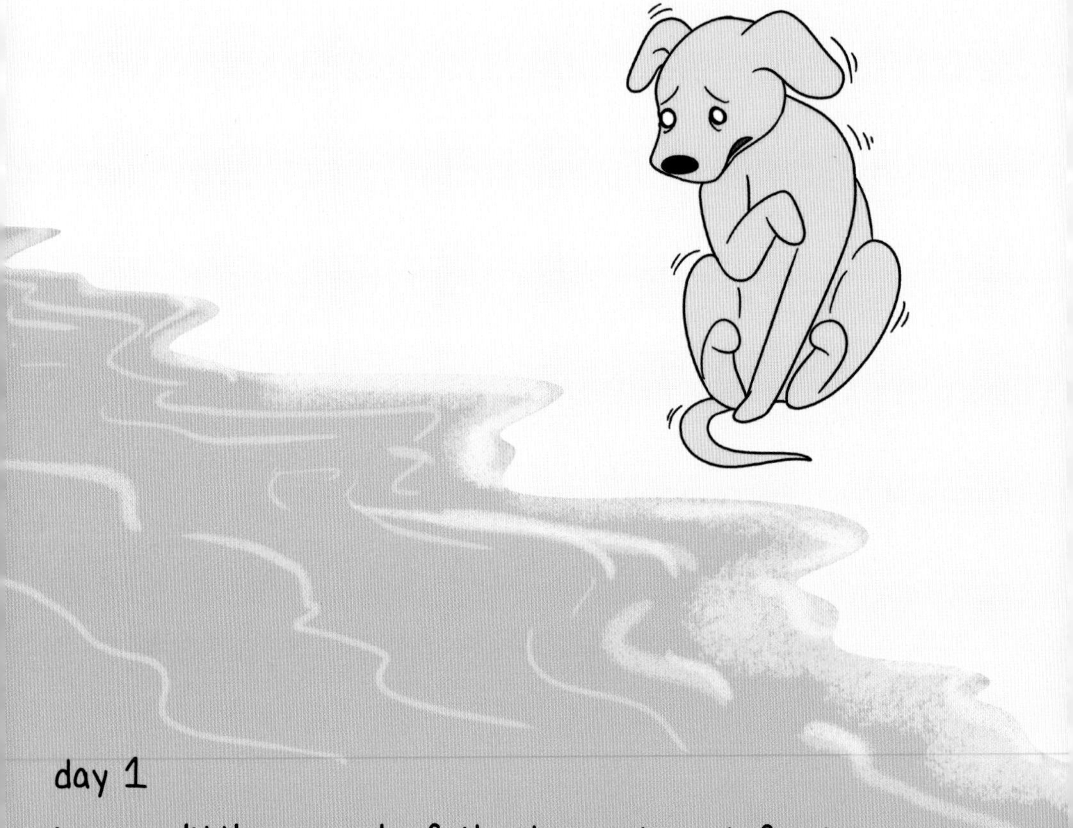

day 1

i was a little scared of the big water at first.

sometimes it would get close to me without asking.

but the human dipped sebastian's feet in. and he didn't seem to mind. so i think it's going to be ok

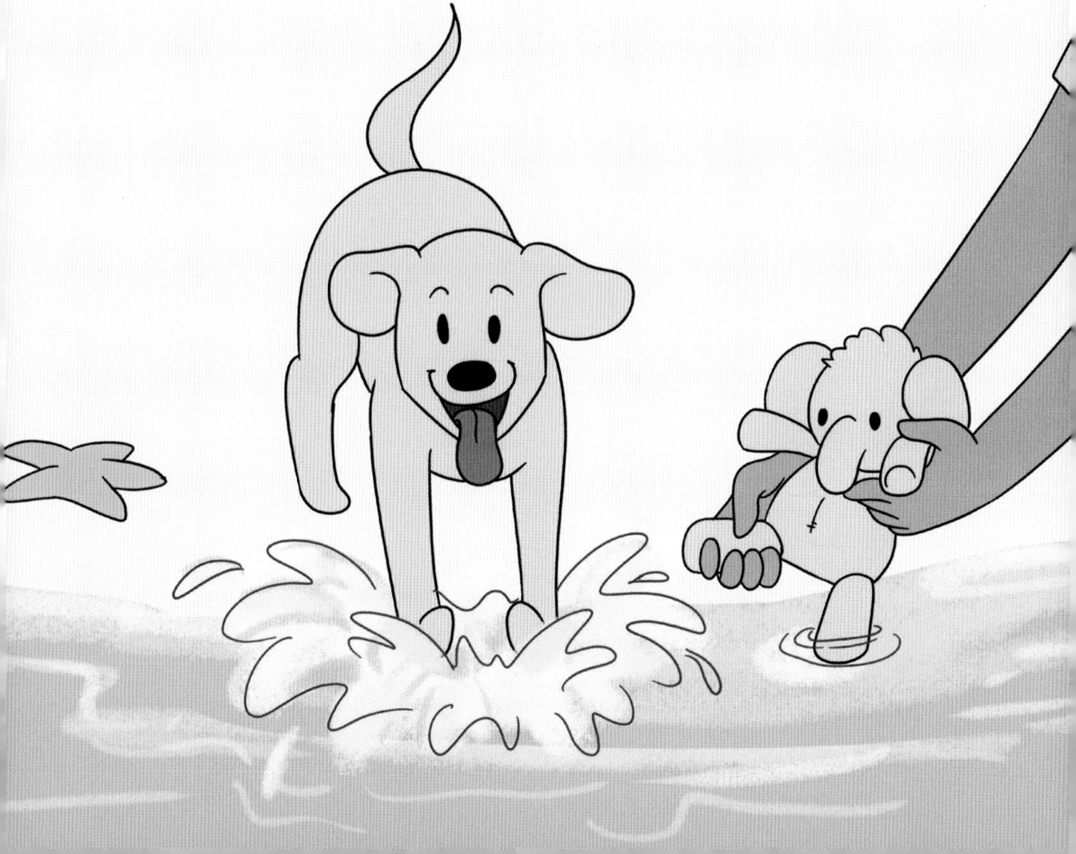

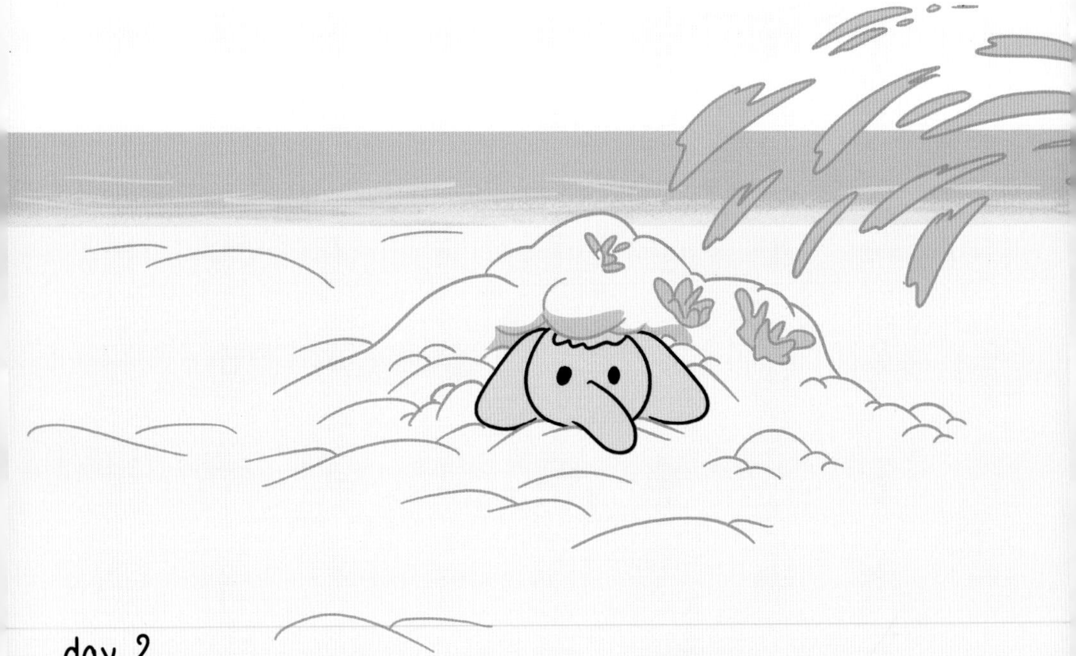

day 2

i accidentally buried my stuffed fren sebastian in the sand.

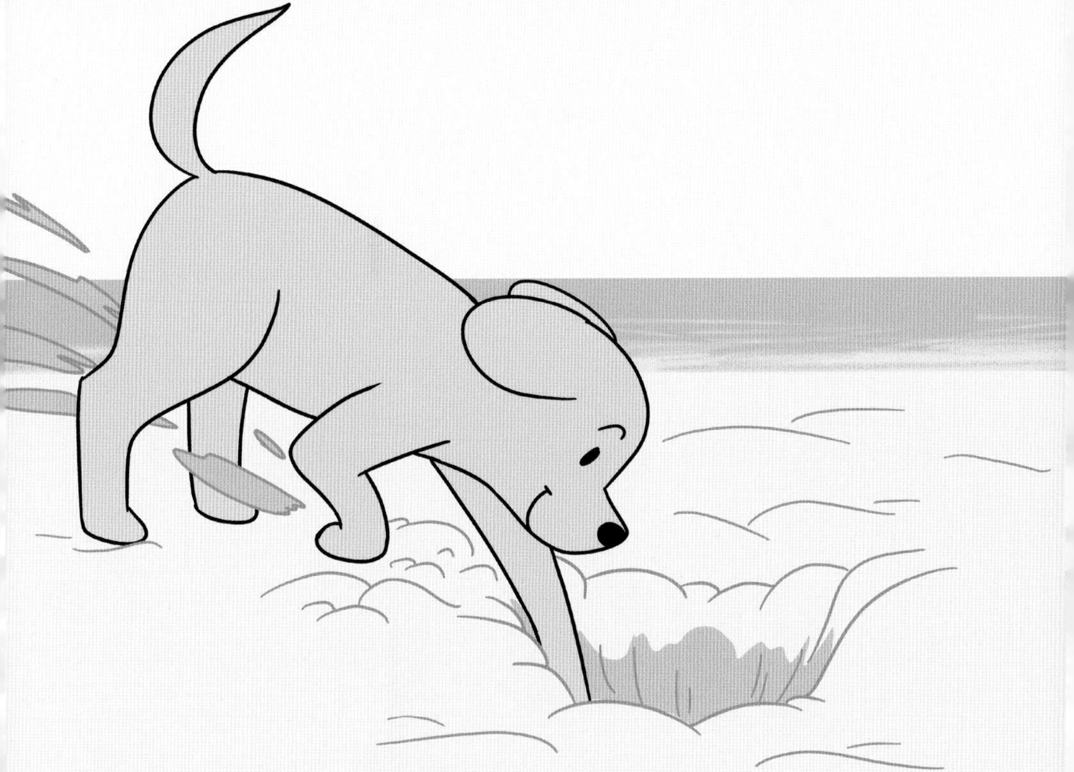

i just wanted to dig a hole. but unfortunately he was behind me during this process

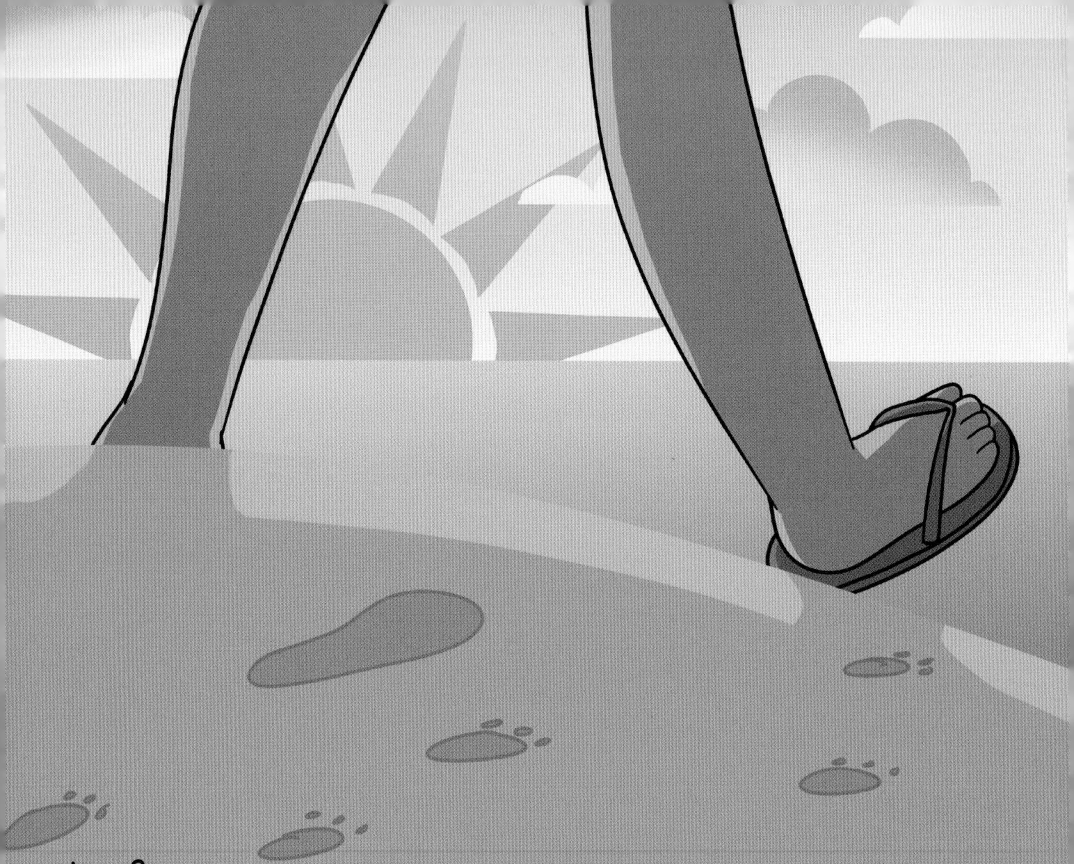

day 3

the human and i went on a walk. alongside the big water. our goal was to pick up all the cool looking seashells.

they will probably set them aside and forget about them later. but that's not my problem. i'm just happy holding the bucket

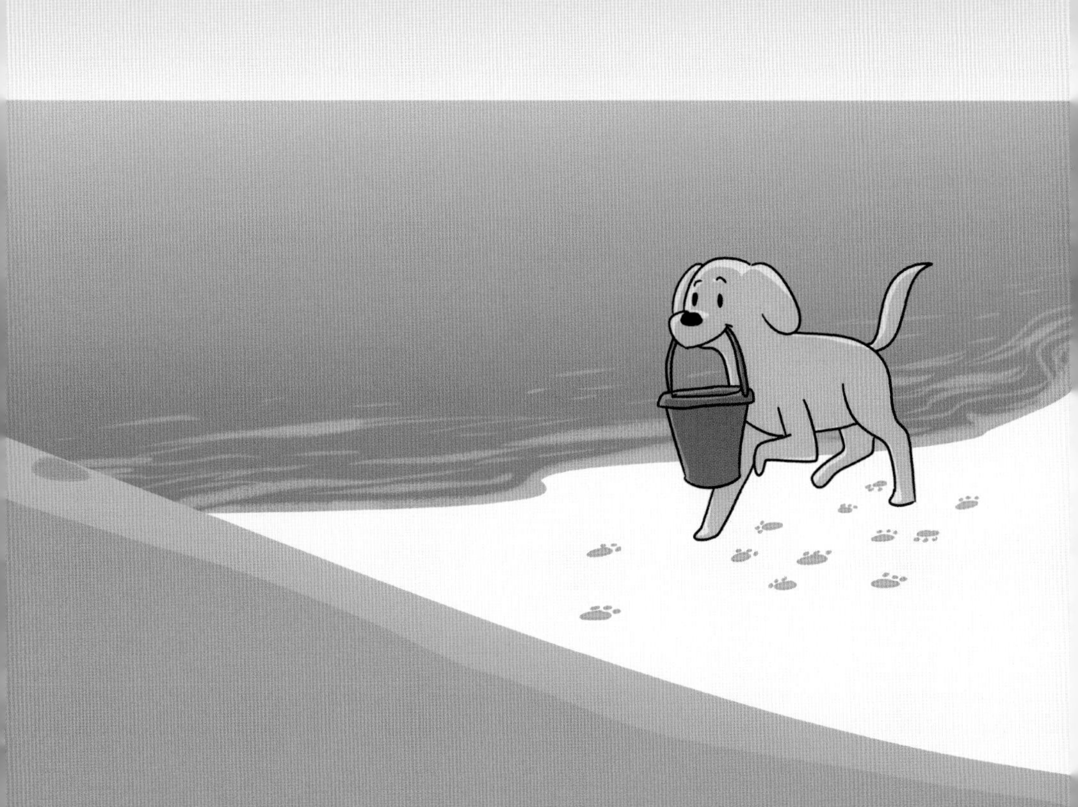

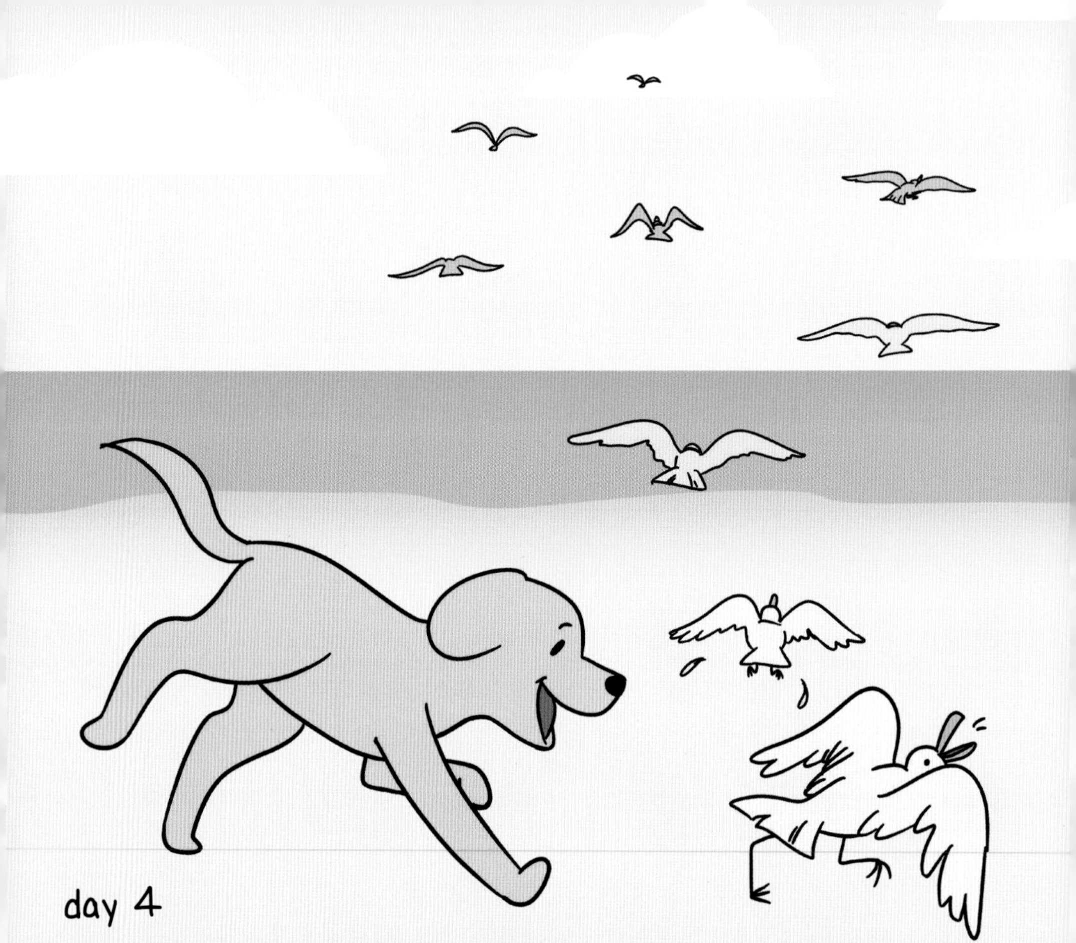

day 4

several large birbs. attempted to steal the human's beach sandwich today.

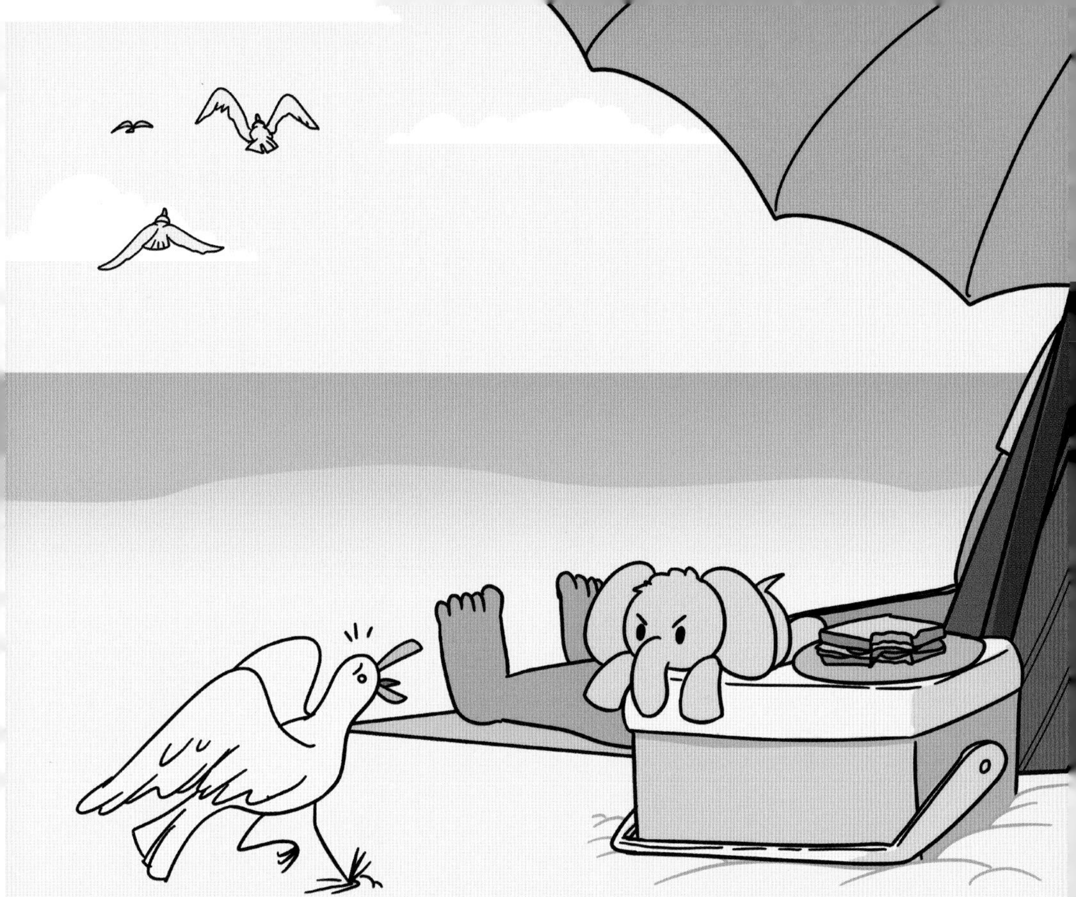

luckily my stuffed fren sebastian and i. were there to scare them away

day 5

it is our last day at the big water. and the human and i spent all morning. designing the best sandcastle ever.

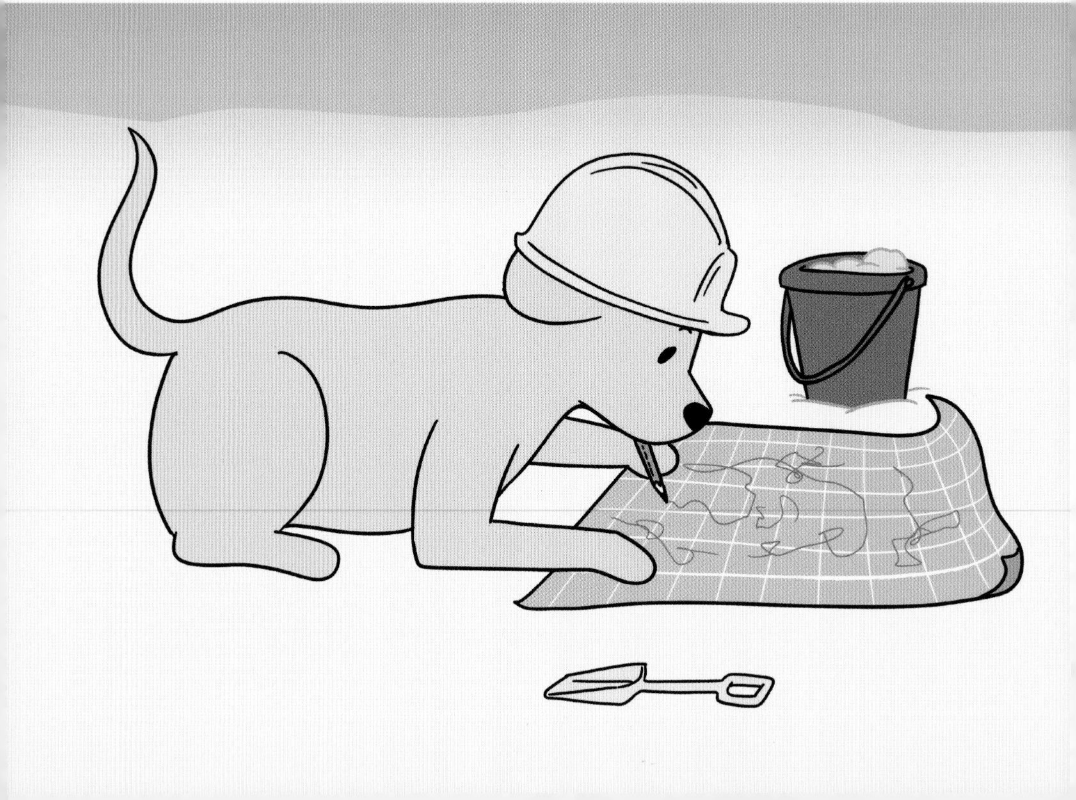

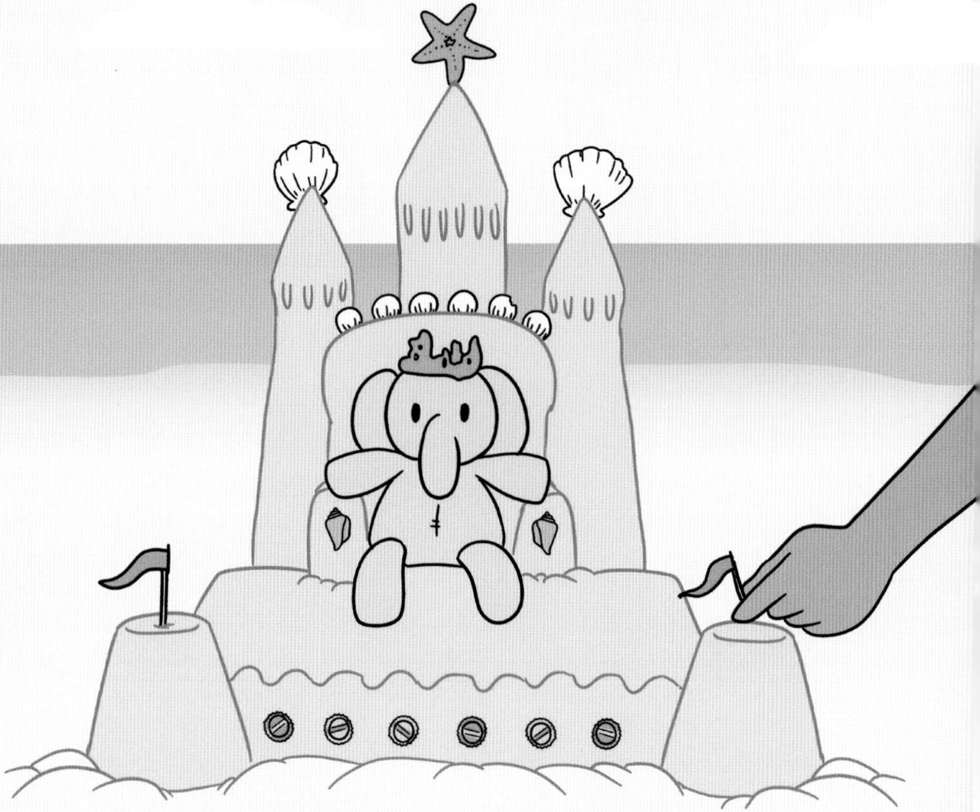

there's even a little throne. for my stuffed fren sebastian. he plans to rule benevolently

4th of July

in the middle of the summer. there are always sky booms. some of which are human made. these ones are usually contained to a single day. sky booms that do not occur on this single day. should never be tolerated

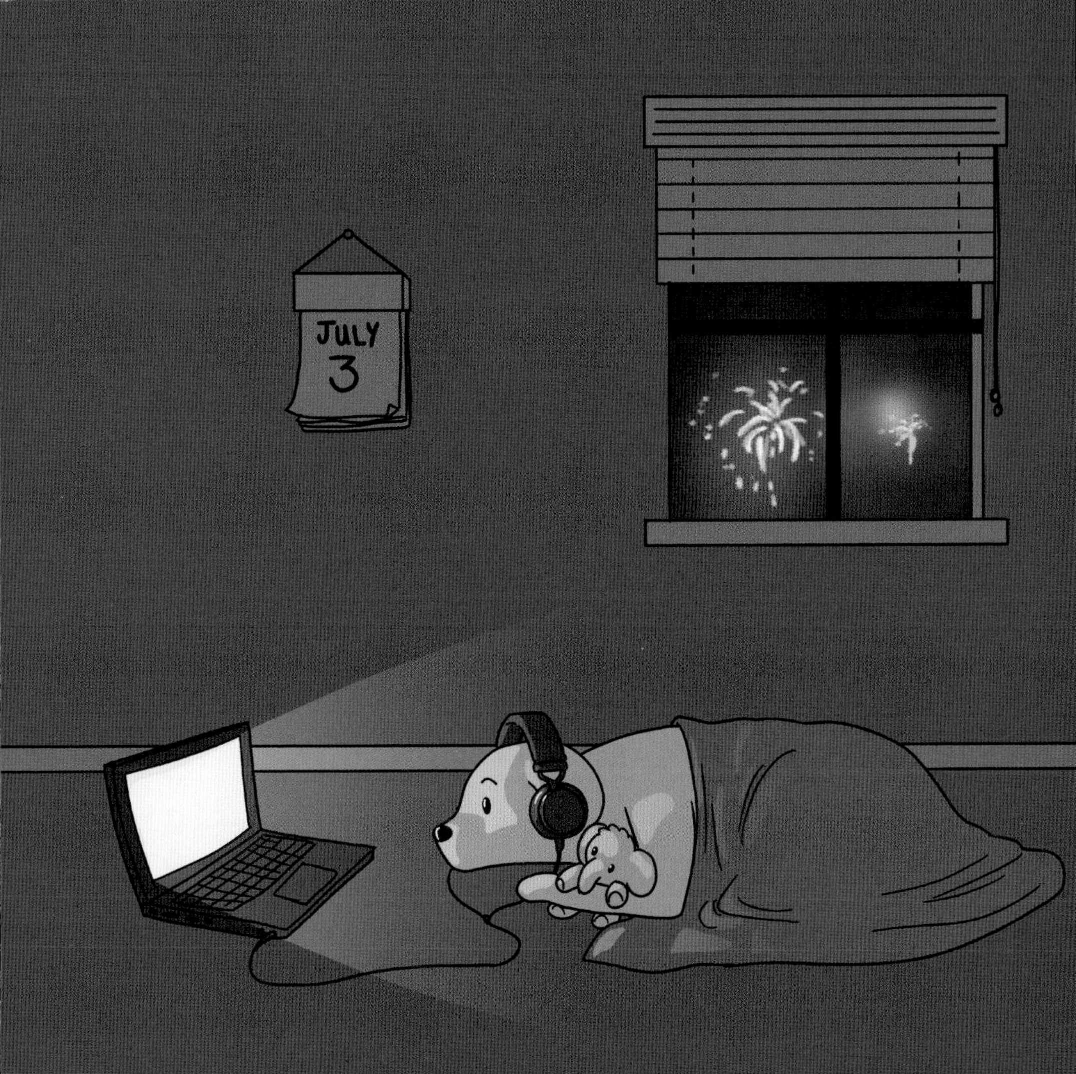
JULY
3

the sky booms have begun. so the human and i are
headed to the shelter. to comfort some pups who
don't yet have. someone to hold them. i made sure to
bring my stuffed fren sebastian. he helps everyone
feel better

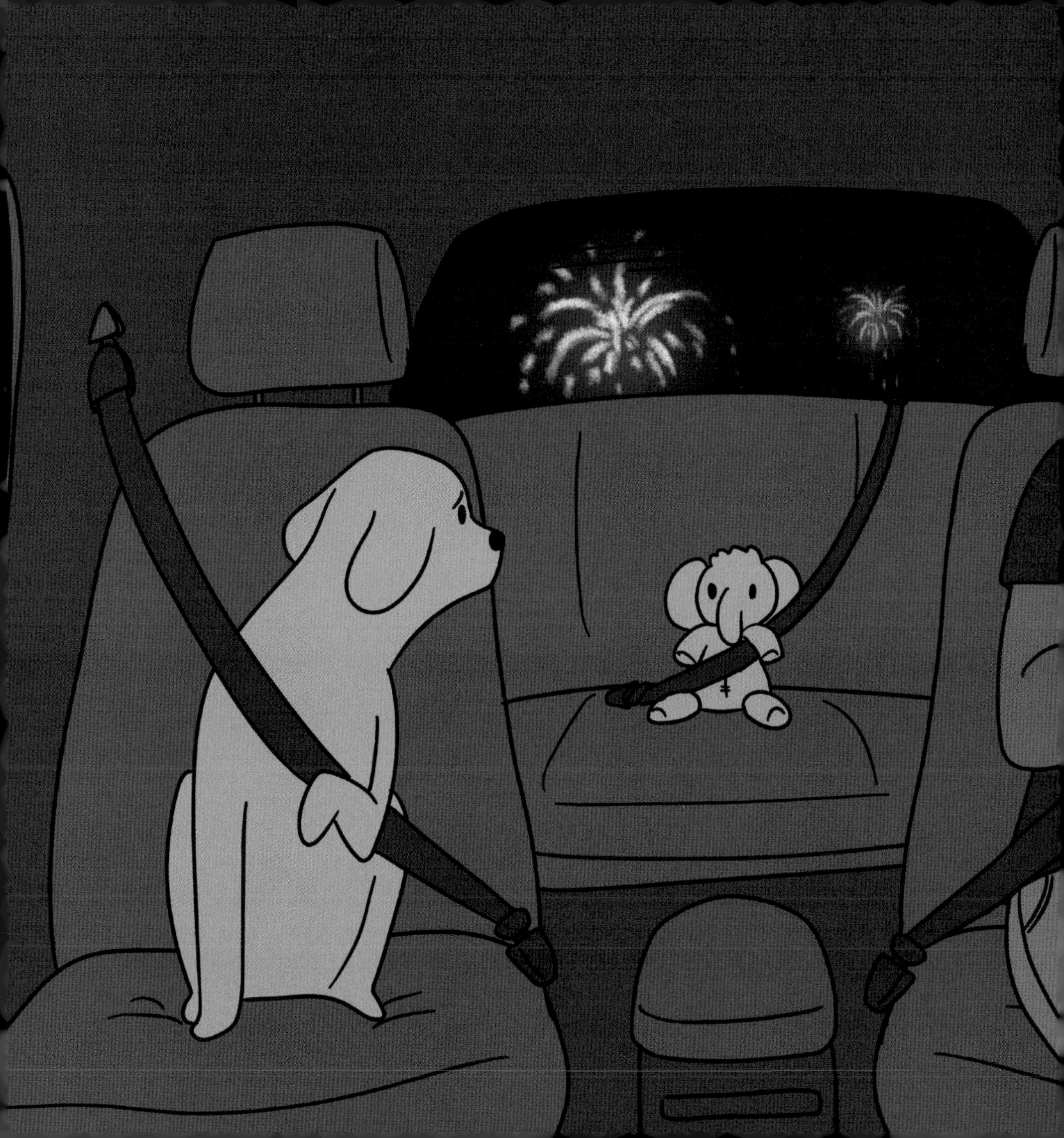

ere allowed to get into the kennels with a few of

n. the human would let them sit in their lap.

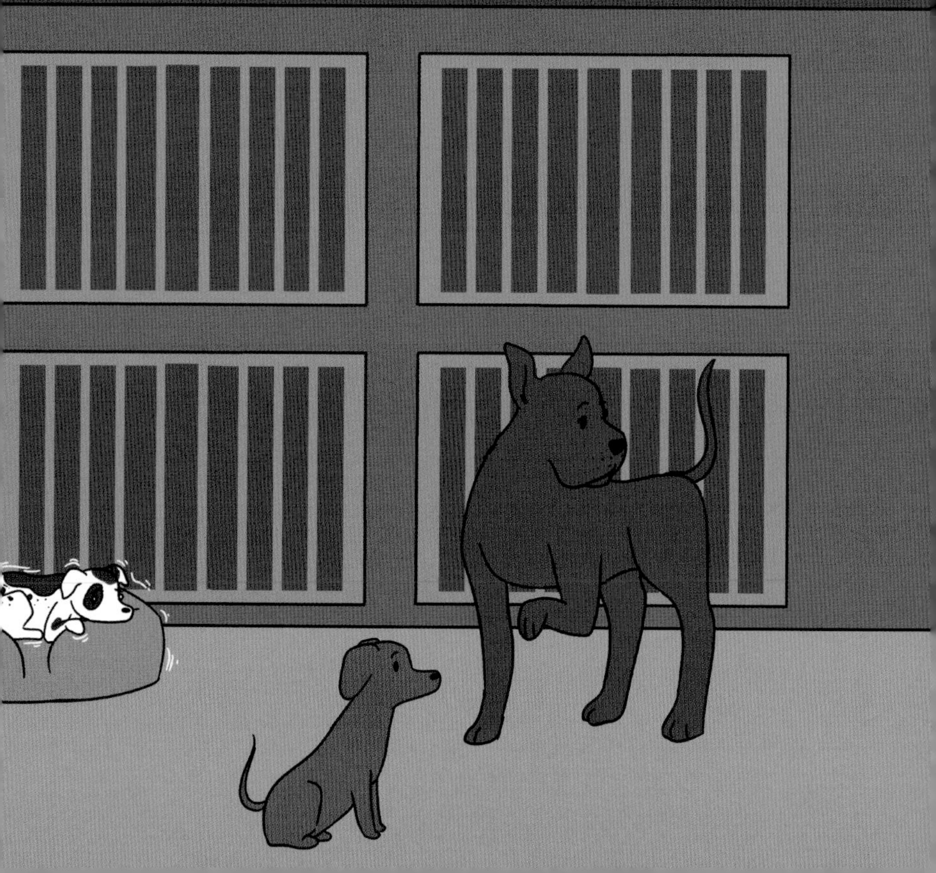

and i would show them sebastian. after a few moments. nobody noticed the sky booms anymore

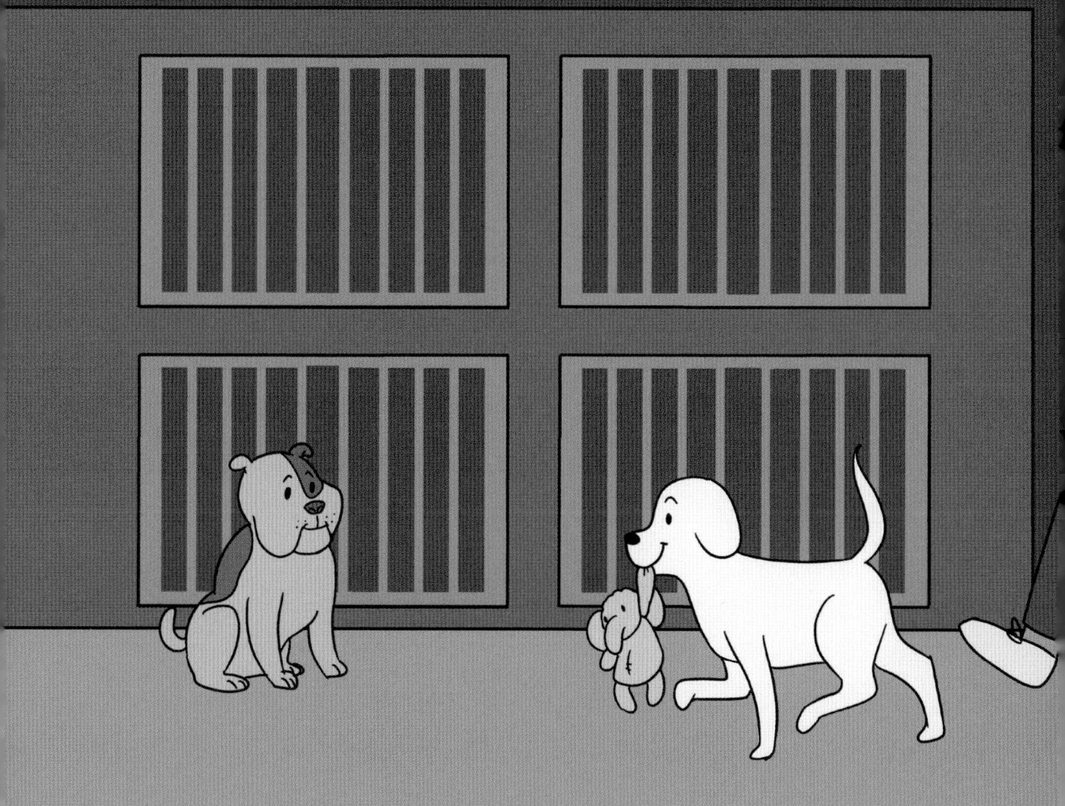

there was one pup. who couldn't stop shaking. so we spent most of the night with them. their name was oreo. and they only calmed down. when they got to hold my stuffed fren sebastian

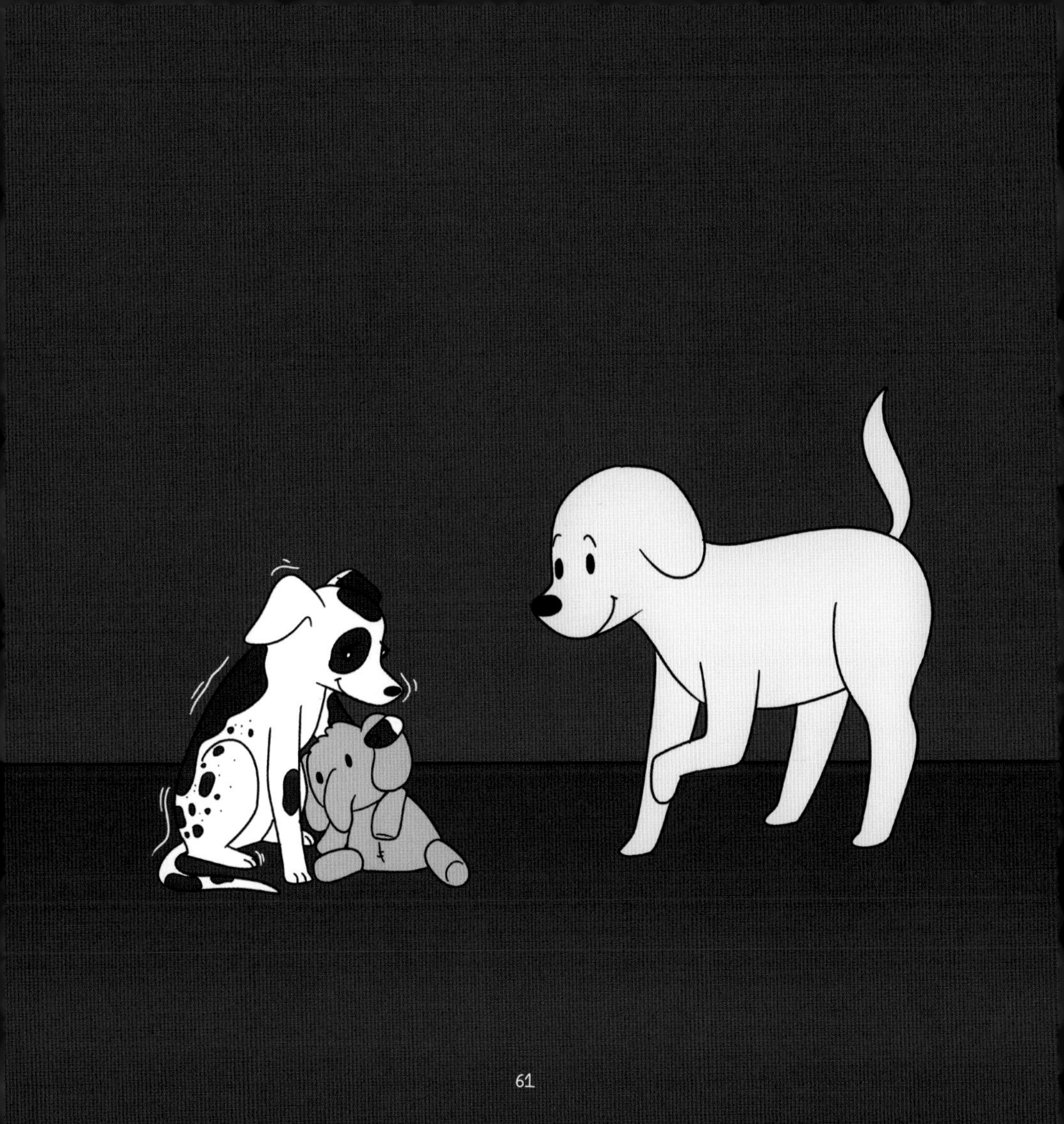

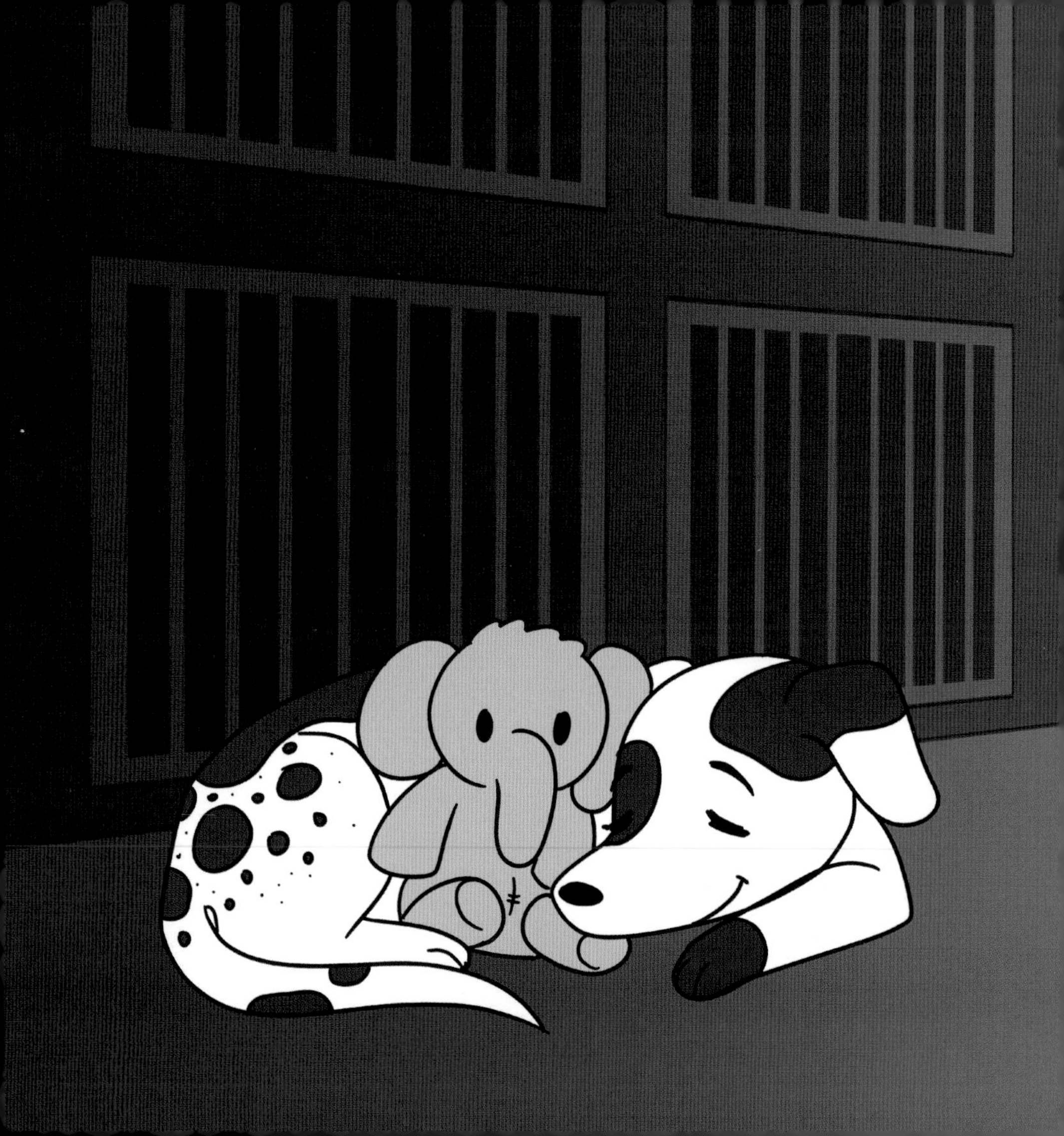

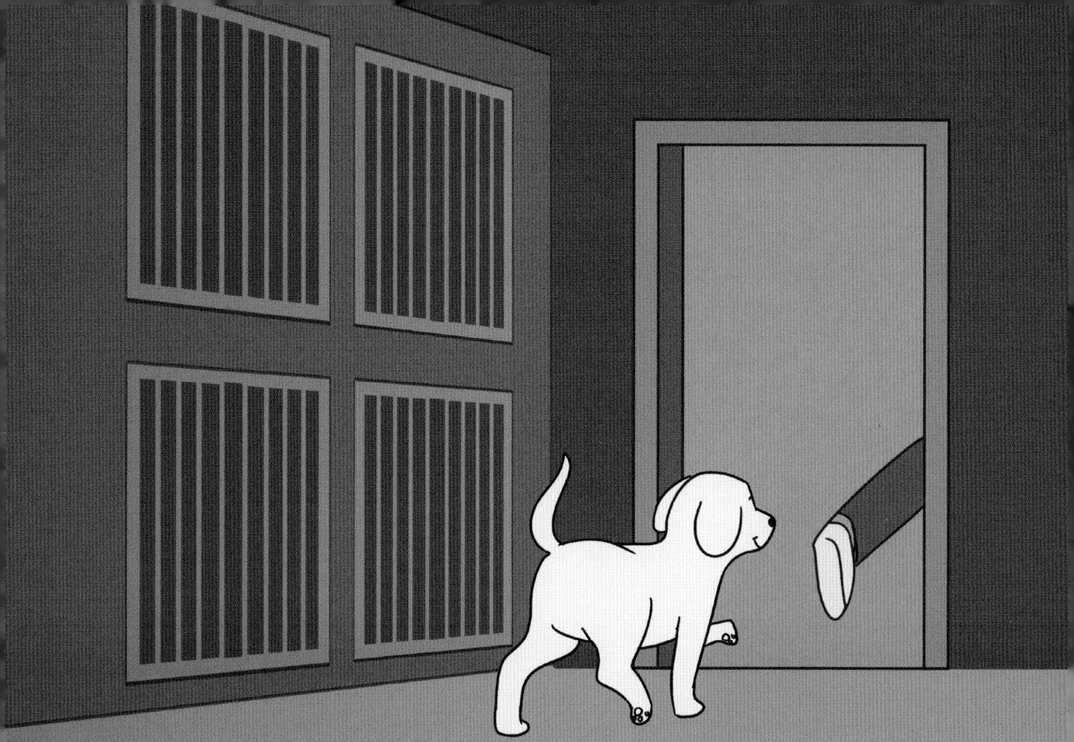

when the sky booms finally stopped. and it was time to go. i left my stuffed fren sebastian with oreo. they needed him more than me. the human said we could pick him back up. first thing in the morning

Arm Falls Off

i was playing with my stuffed fren sebastian. when his arm fell all the way off. i remember the first time this happened. i was nearly inconsolable.

but now i know there's no need to worry. because among many other things. my human is a surgeon

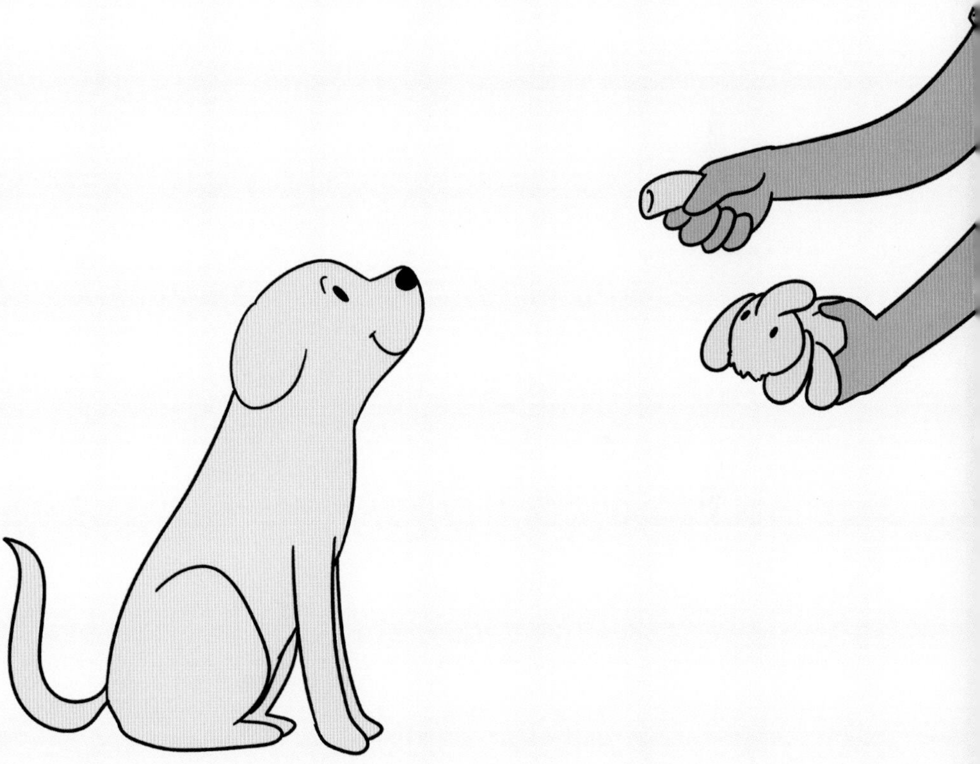

they have a magical kit. equipped with all the necessary belongings. and i sit right beside them. as they put sebastian back together again

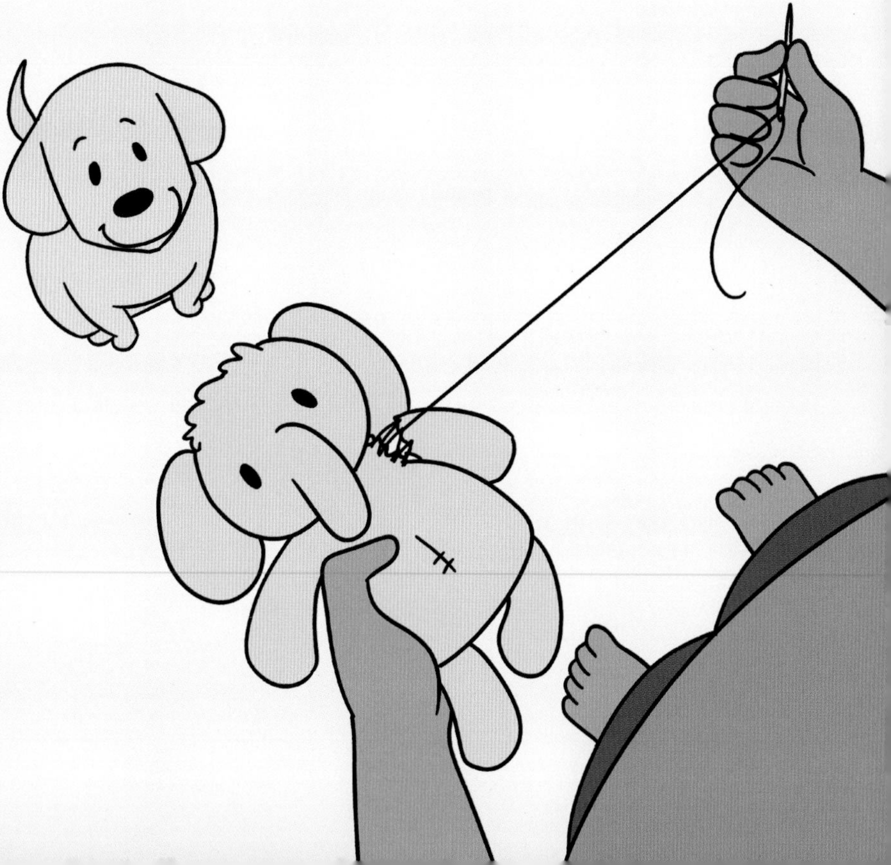

sebastian does a wonderful job remaining calm. but i always offer my paw. in case he wants to hold it. it's important to let him know. i'm not going anywhere

within the hour. my stuffed fren sebastian was out of surgery. and whole once more. i think i'll carry him by the other arm from now on

Halloween

we have entered spooky season. so we are all headed to the pumpkin patch. and although i've been told. i can only bring one home. i am going to say hi. to every pumpkin i see

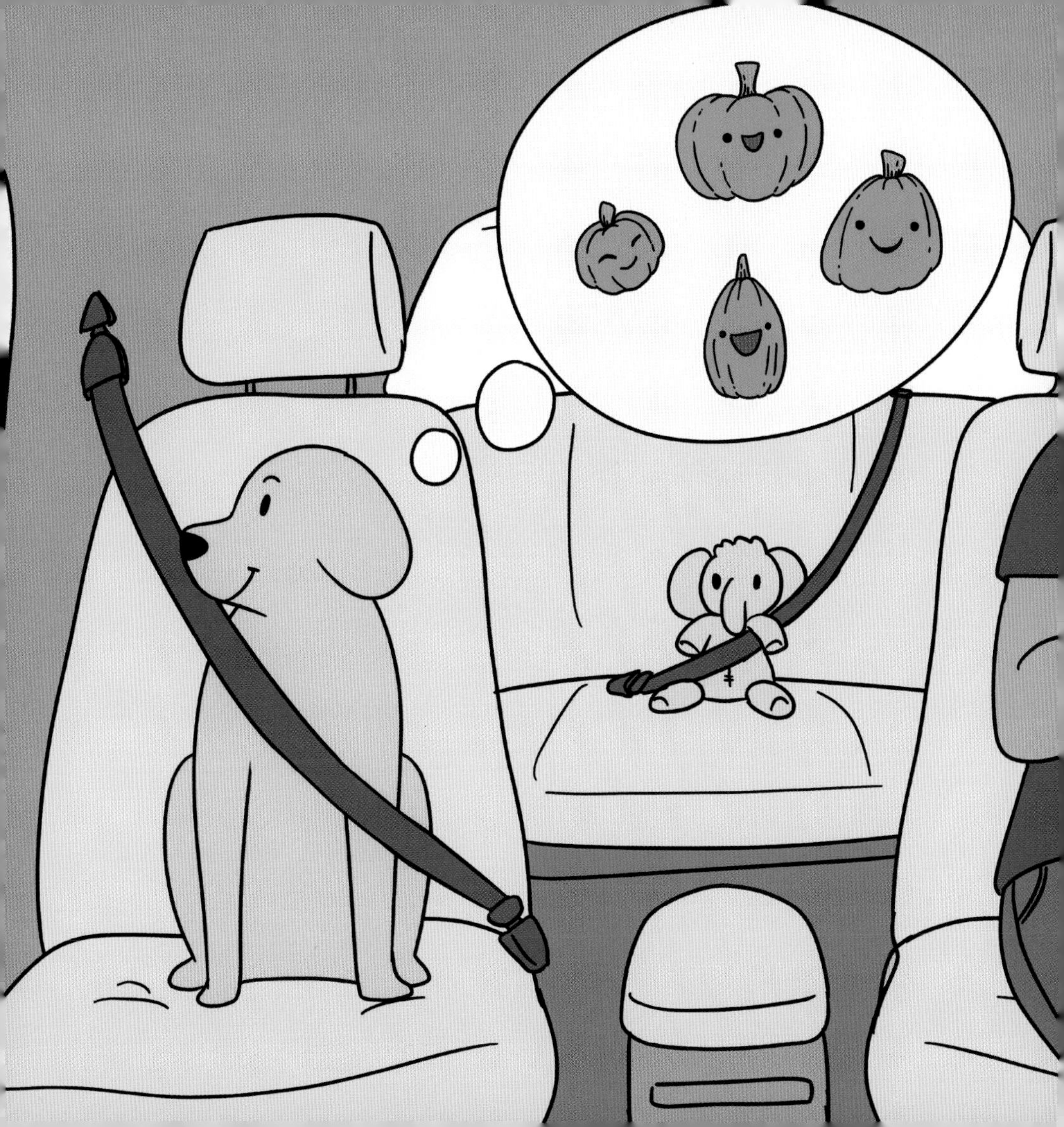

there were many perfect pumpkins. but my stuffed fren sebastian and i. decided to get a lopsided one. with a broken stem. and a few bruises.

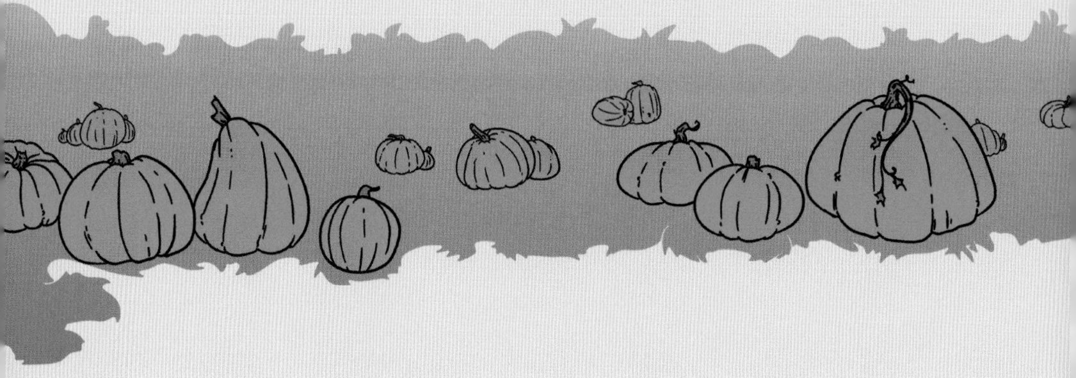

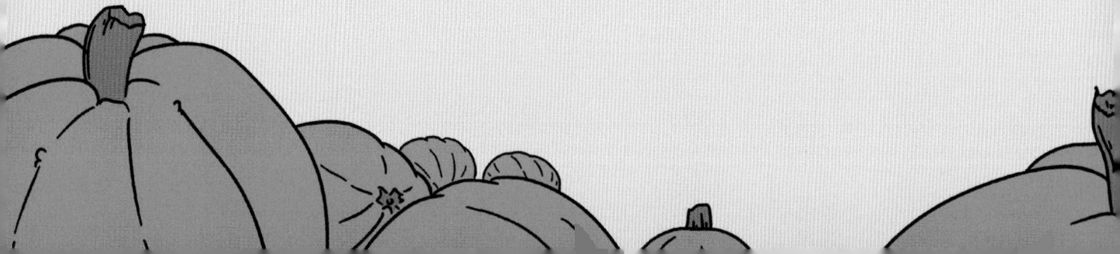

because we have a lot of love to give.
and this one needed all of it

we've been keeping our new pumpkin fren. outside during the day.

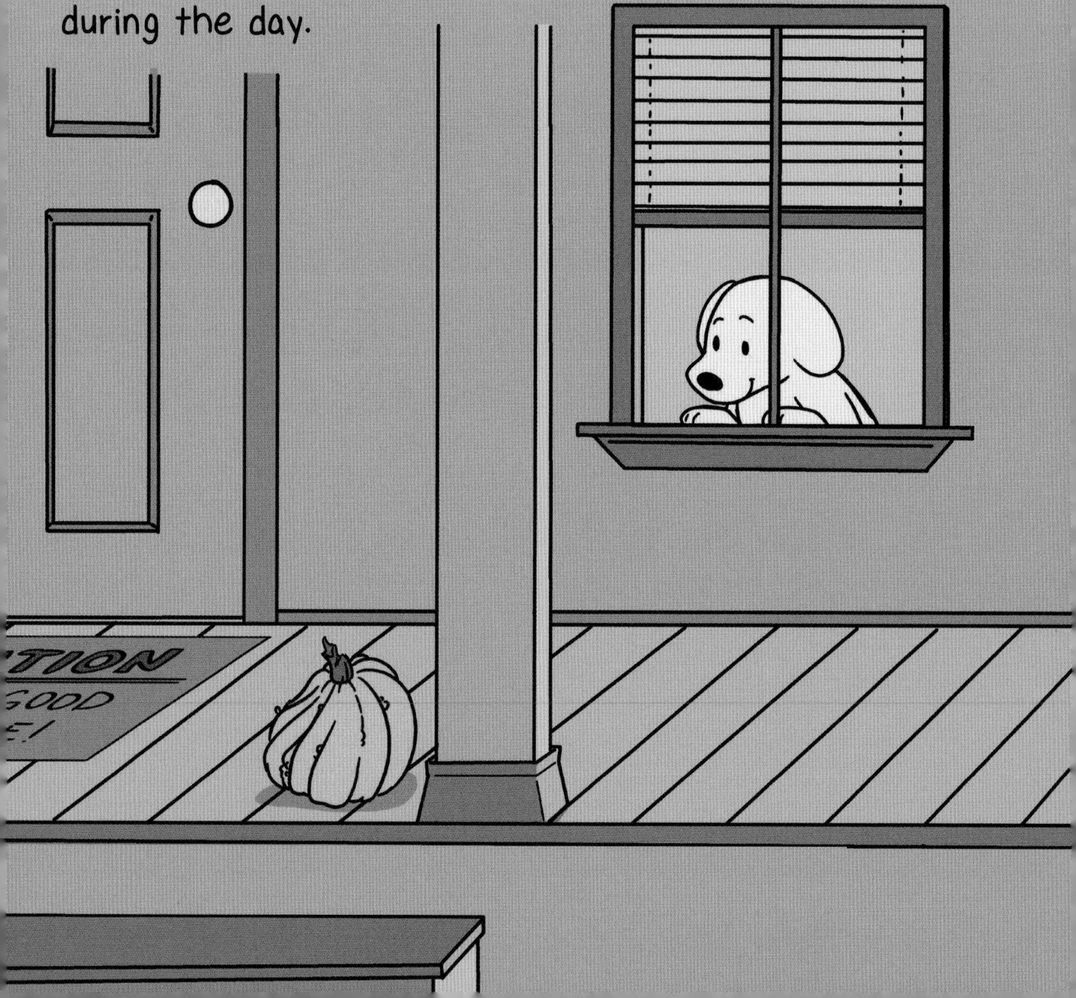
TION
GOOD
E!

but before i go to bed. i make the human bring them inside. because it can get cold out there. and they deserve to be cozy

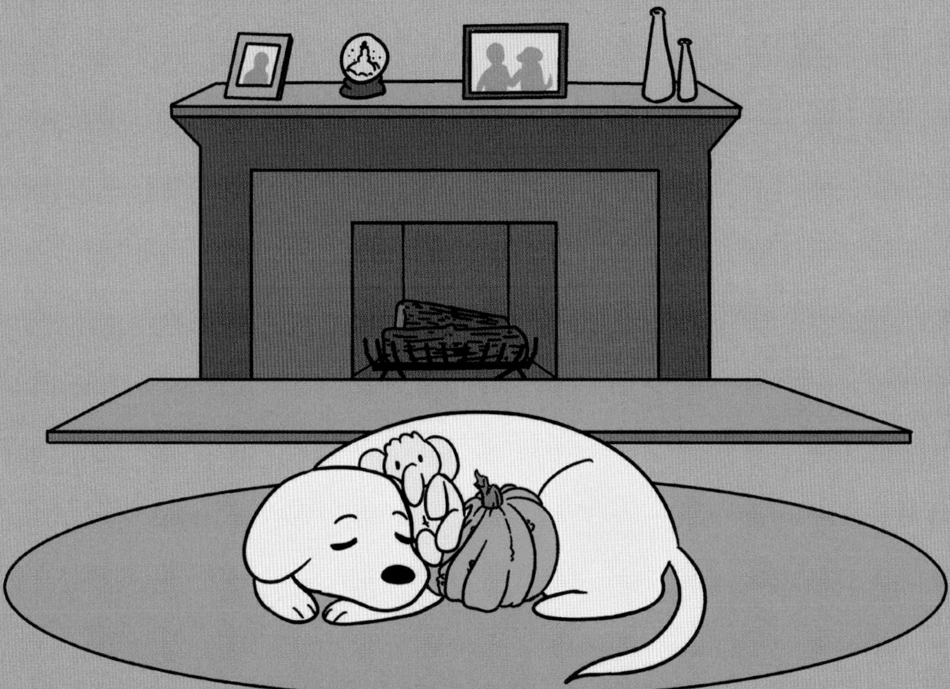

today was pumpkin carving day. but i am already very
attached to my pumpkin. so when it was time to carve.
i didn't let anyone near them.

i saved them from the knife. and in the pumpkin realm.
i am a hero

i've given my stuffed fren sebastian. a little ghost costume. his job is to make sure. i receive all the pats i deserve. when we give out the candy later

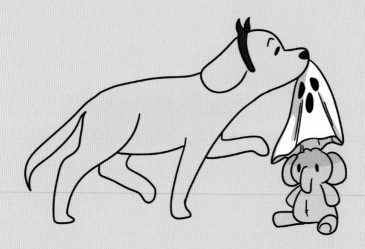

the human says each tiny monster. only gets two pieces. but i can't count. so that's not my rule to enforce

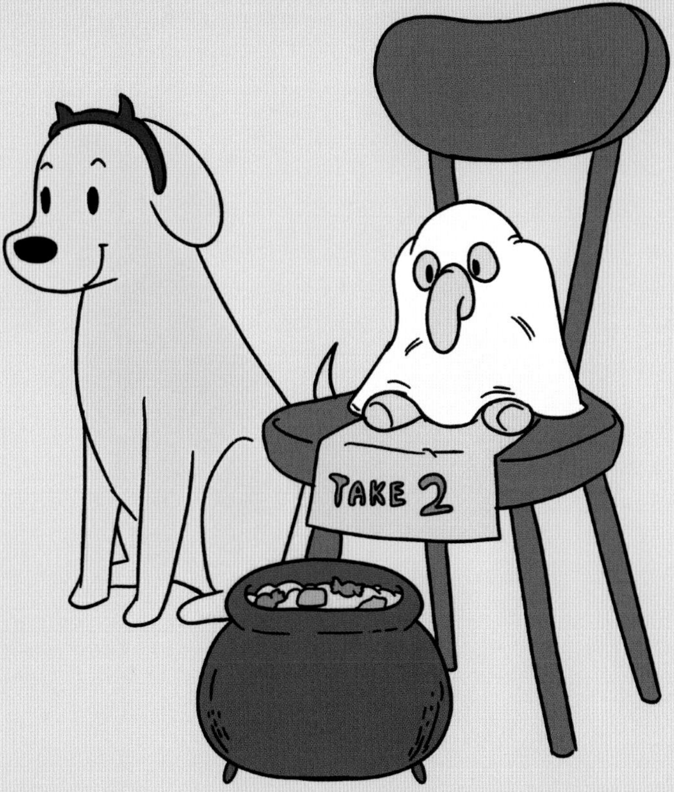
TAKE 2

the tiny monsters are finally here. and my job. is to hold the bucket of candy for them. i'm not allowed to have any myself. but i expect many noggin pats for my services. and those are just as sweet

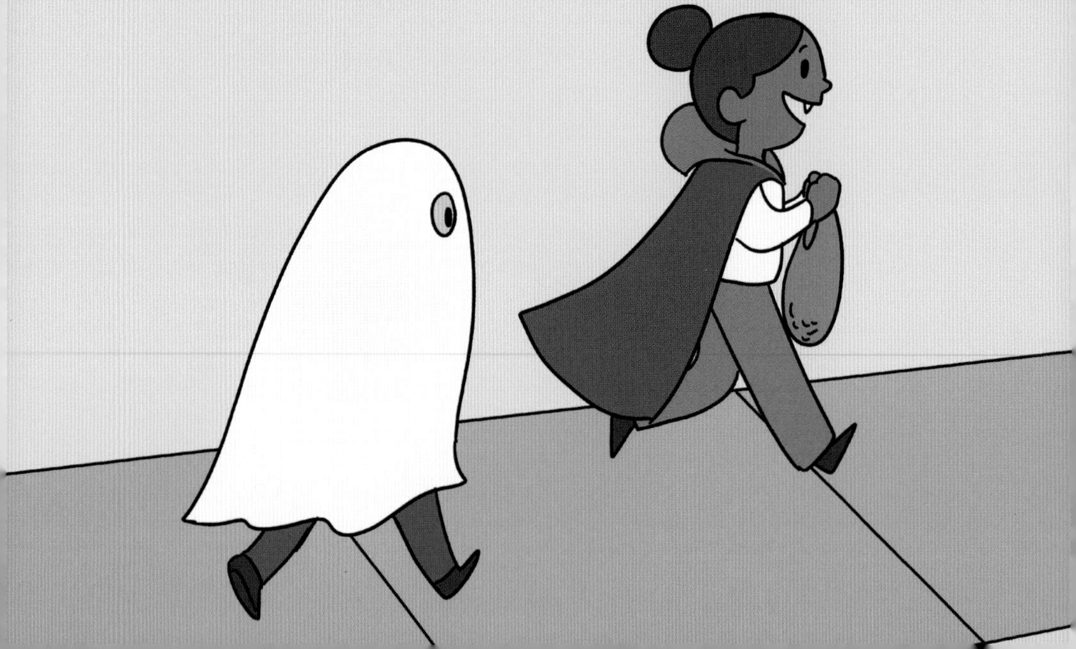

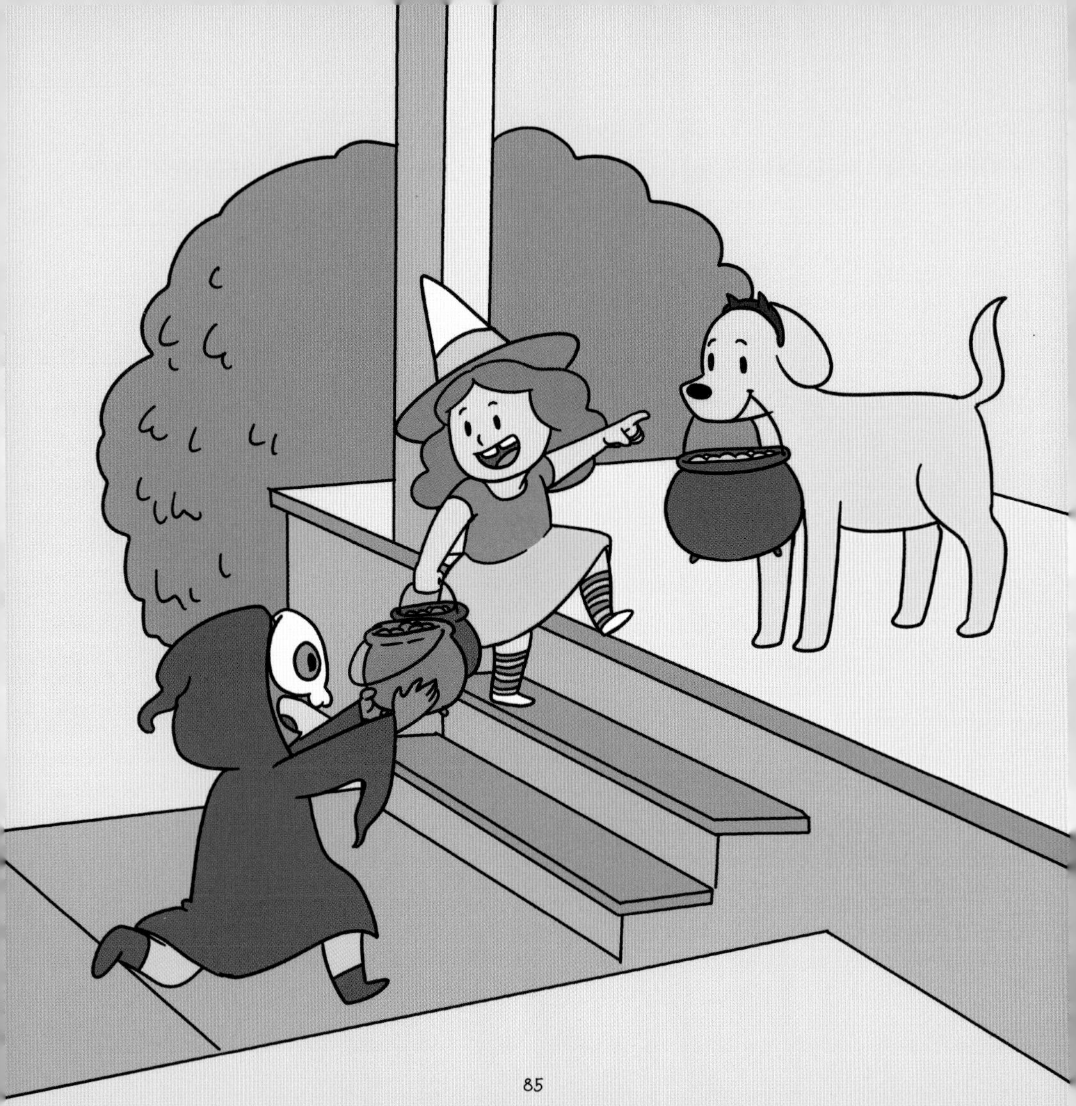

the tiny monsters saw my pumpkin. and wondered why
they're not carved into something fun. but through a
series of noises. i let them know. they're perfect just
the way they are

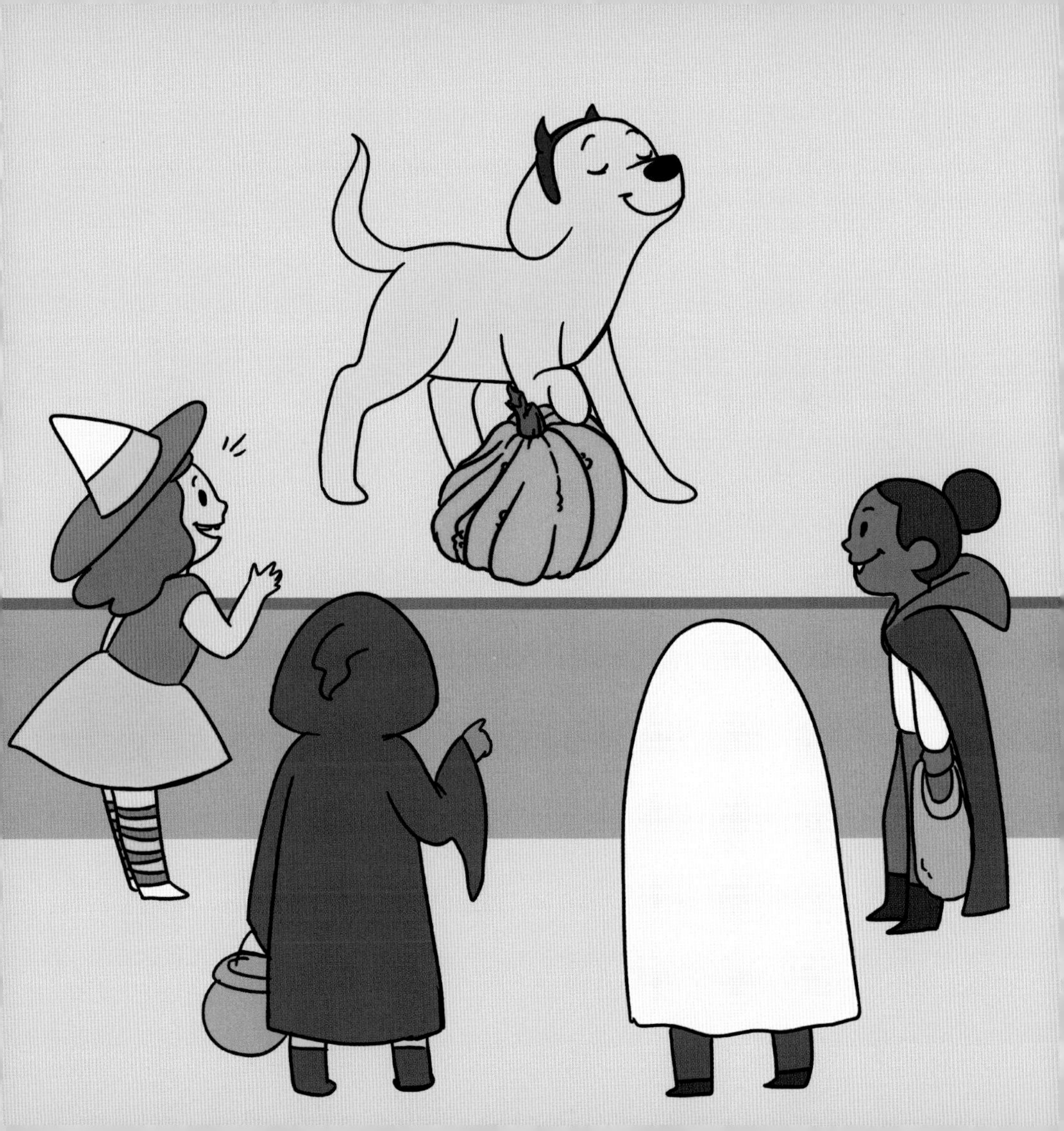

Car Ride

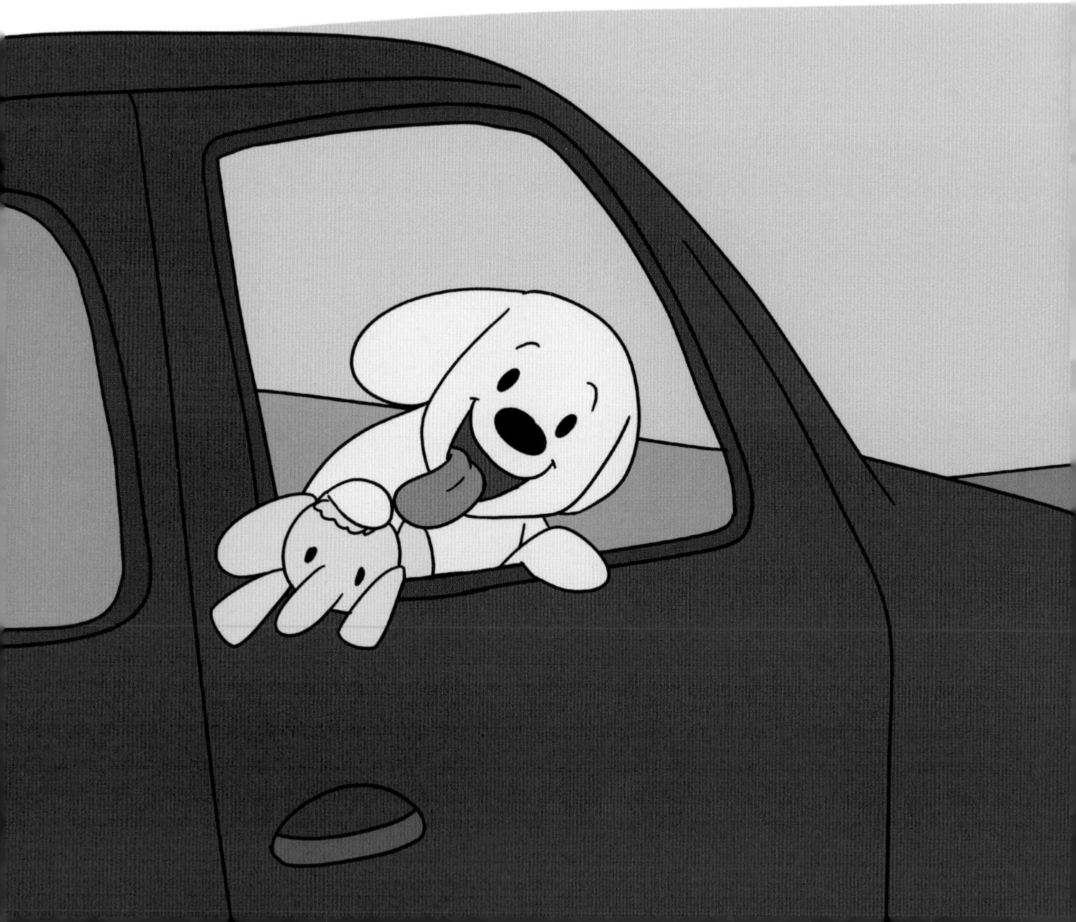

i always bring my stuffed fren sebastian on car rides. because everybody should experience the joy. of sticking their tongue. out of a moving vehicle

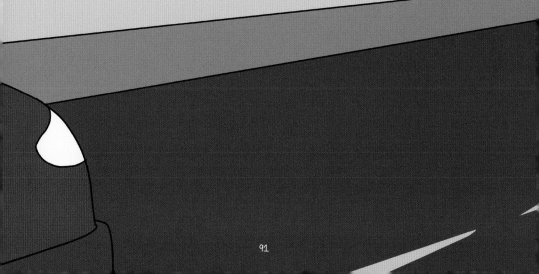

at one specific gray light. we pulled up beside another car. and in the backseat. was a pup just like me

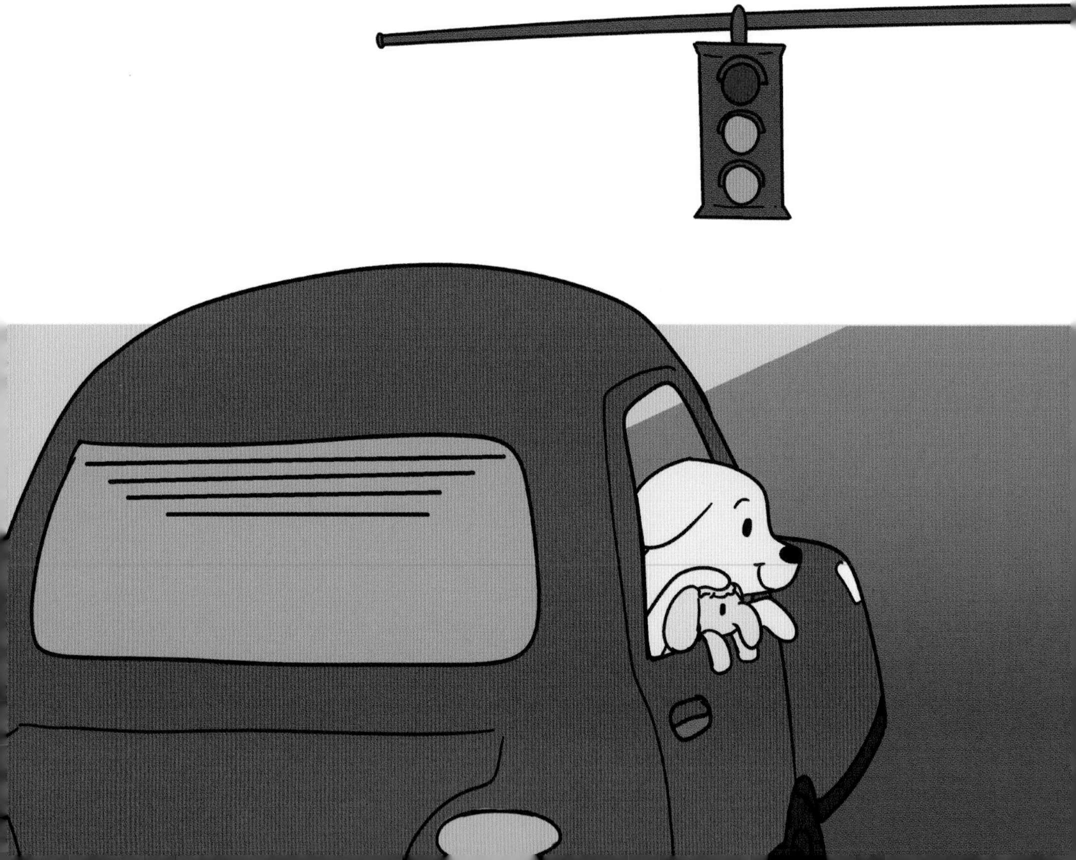

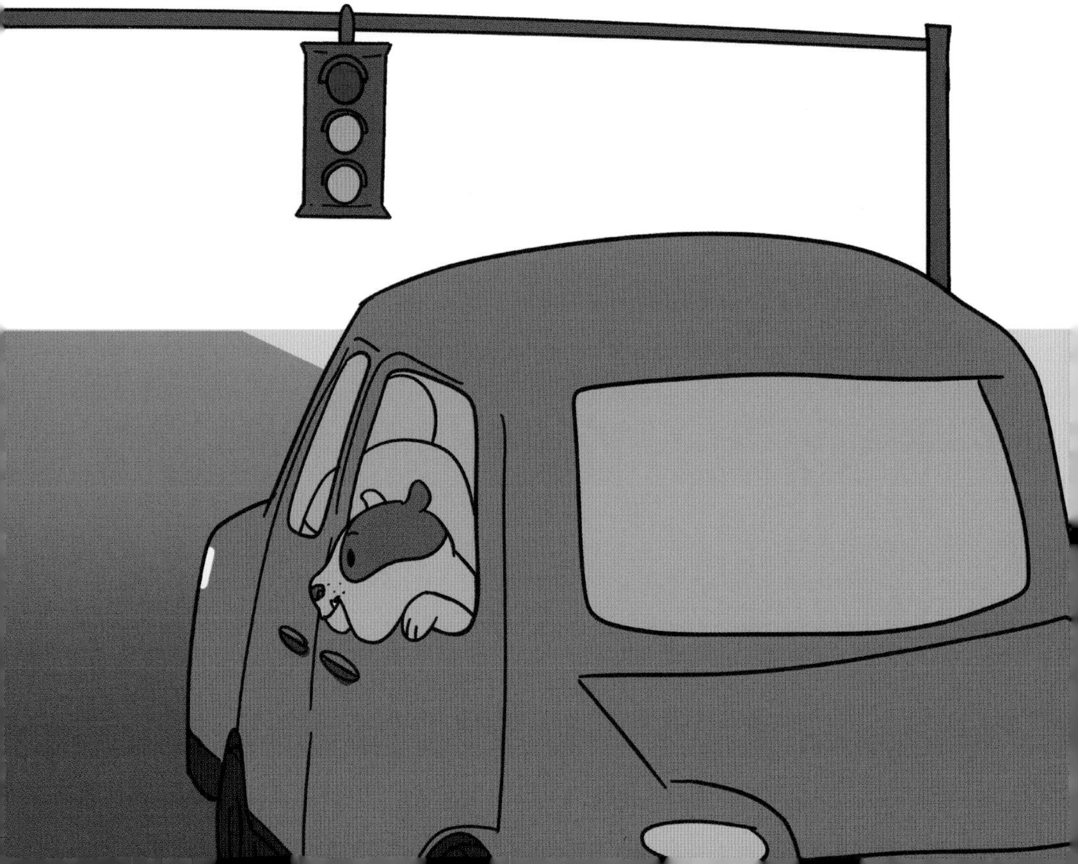

i instructed the human to immediately roll the window all the way down. so i could show this other pup. my stuffed fren sebastian

when they saw sebastian. they disappeared for a moment. before popping back up with their own stuffed fren. theirs was a massive avocado. and by the slobber marks. it was clear they loved it very much

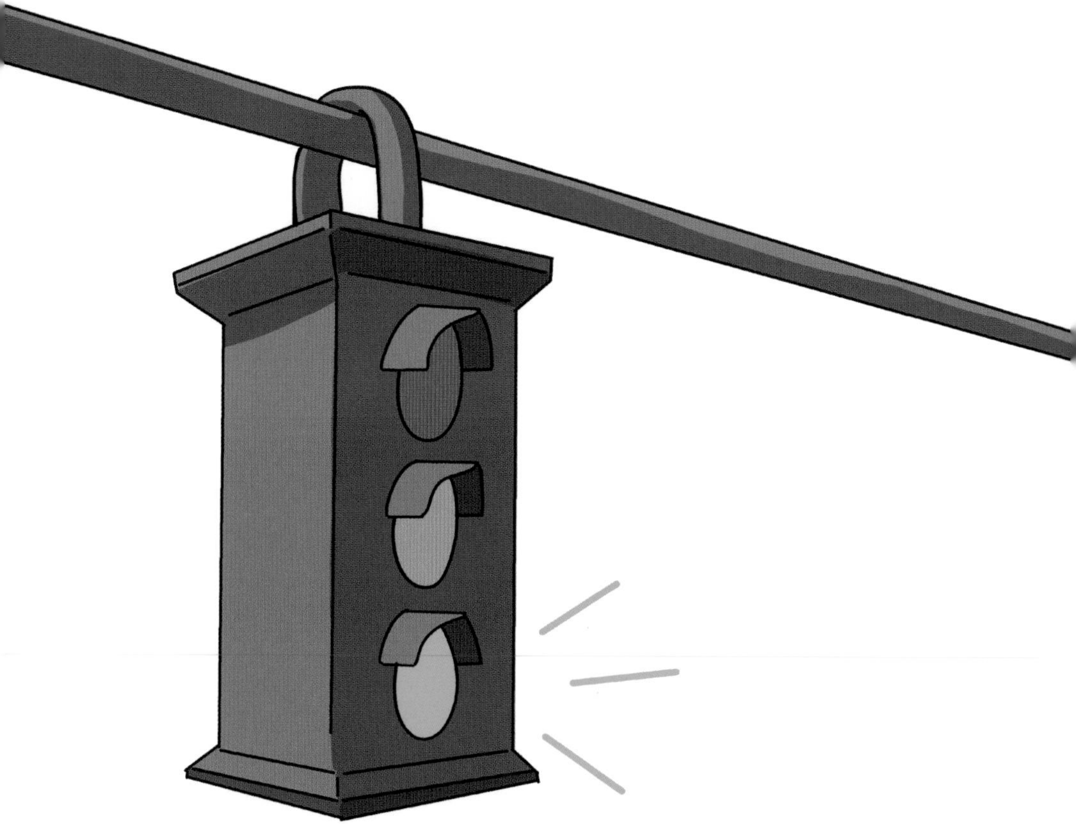

the light switched shortly after. and our cars were quickly separated. but not only did i make a new fren. my new fren's stuffed fren is now my stuffed fren's fren. and that is beautiful

Mailman

i actually look forward to seeing the mailman. because a long time ago. they brought me my stuffed fren sebastian. and i could never thank them enough for doing that

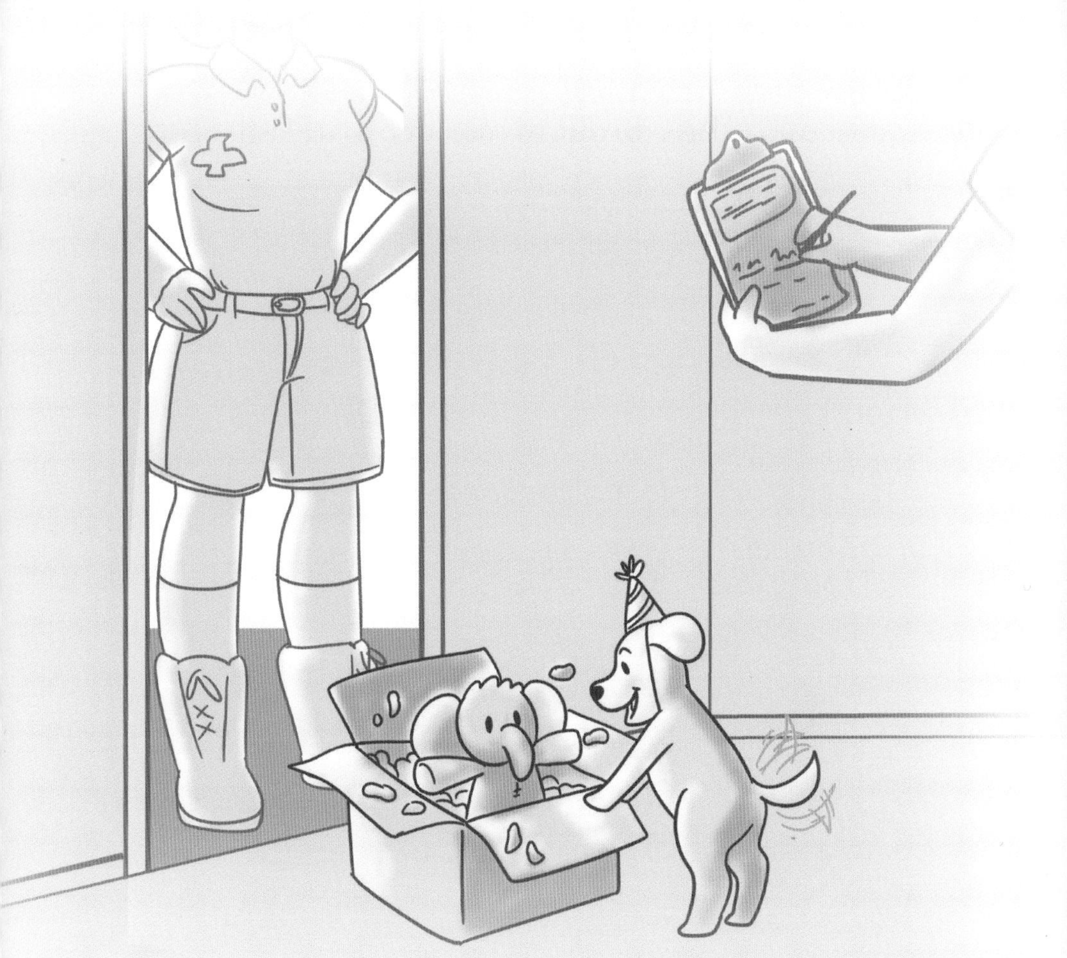

today a new mailman came by the house. so of course i went to the window to say hi. they quickly stepped back

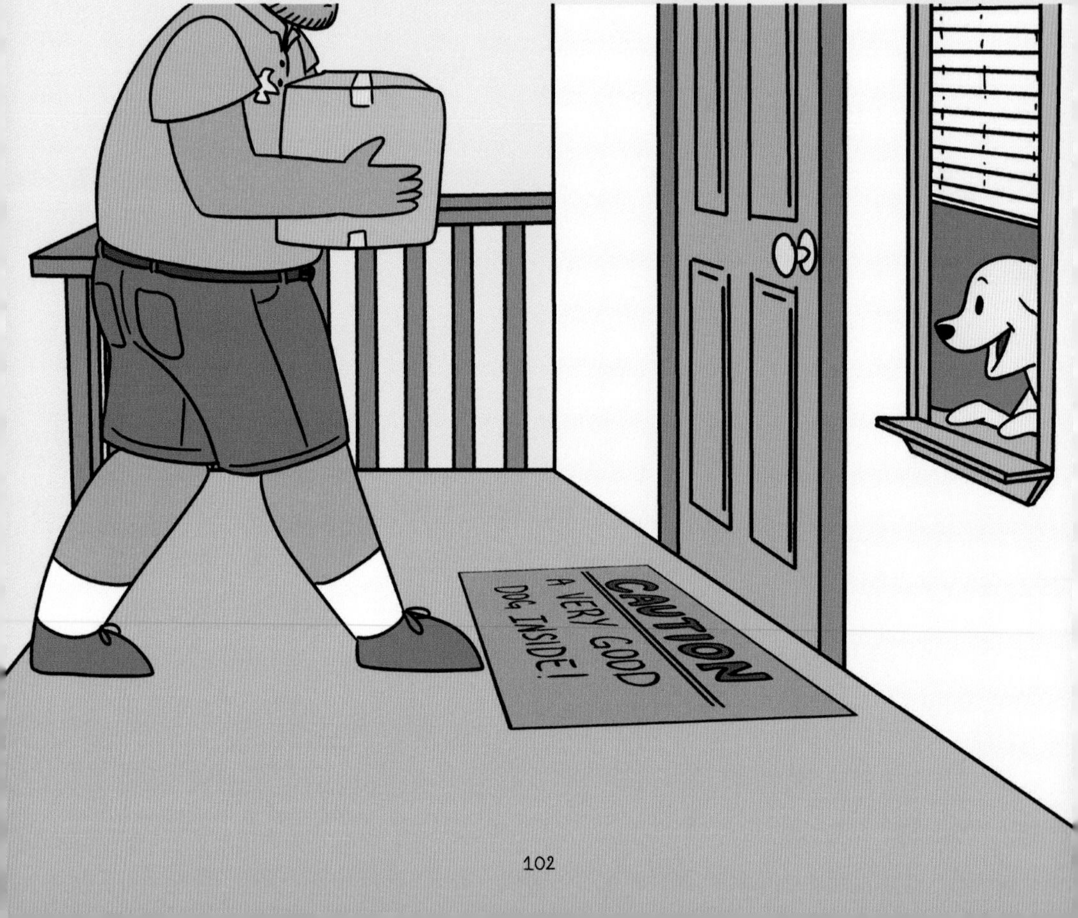
CAUTION
A VERY GOOD
DOG INSIDE!

when they saw me. and hesitantly put the gifts down
before walking away. i'm not sure what i did wrong

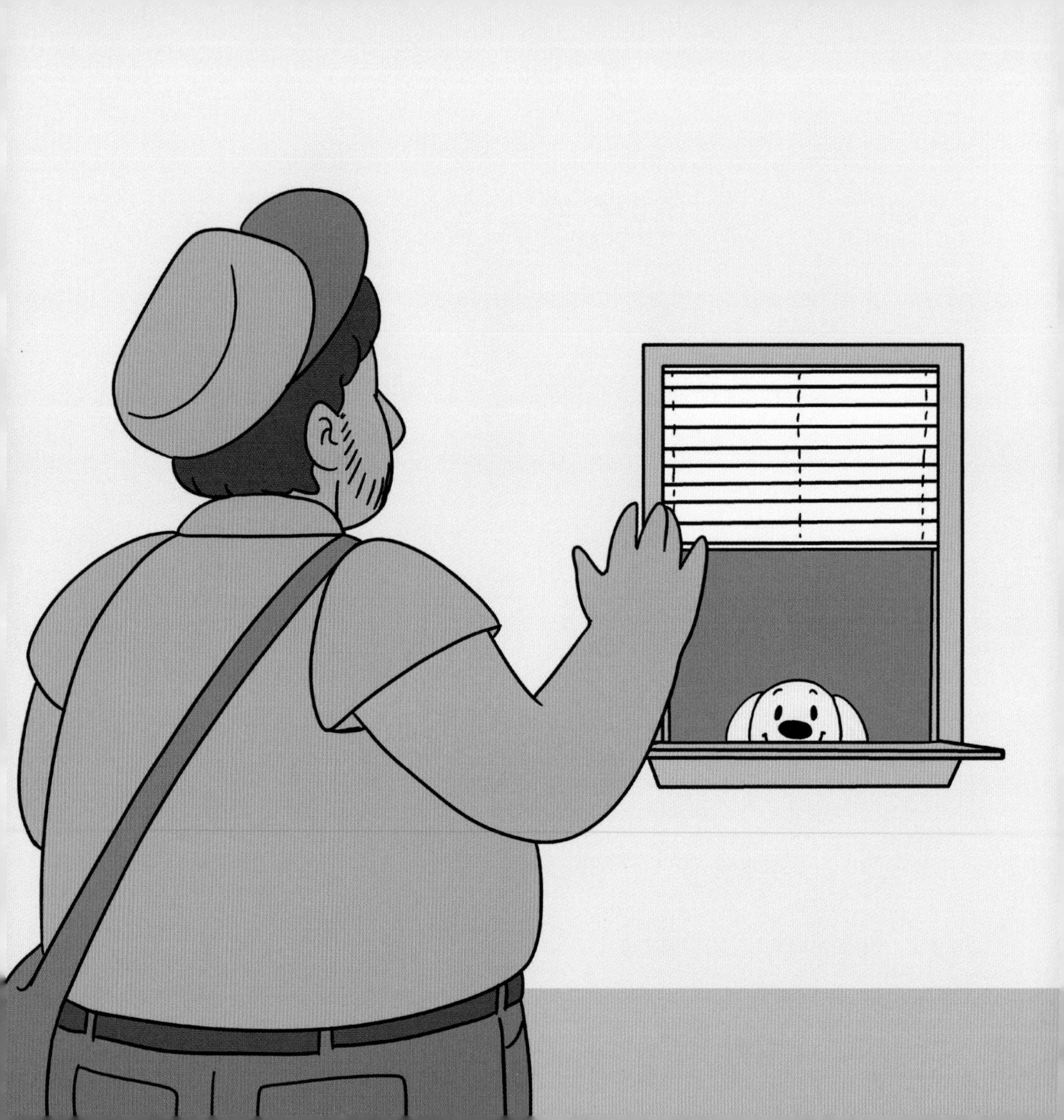

the new mailman is back. and this time i made sure i
didn't surprise them. they were still very quiet. but i'm
pretty sure i saw them smile. as they turned to head
back to the van

today i happened to be outside. when the new mailman arrived. i wasn't sure how they would feel about that. so i sat out of the way. as they dropped off the gifts.

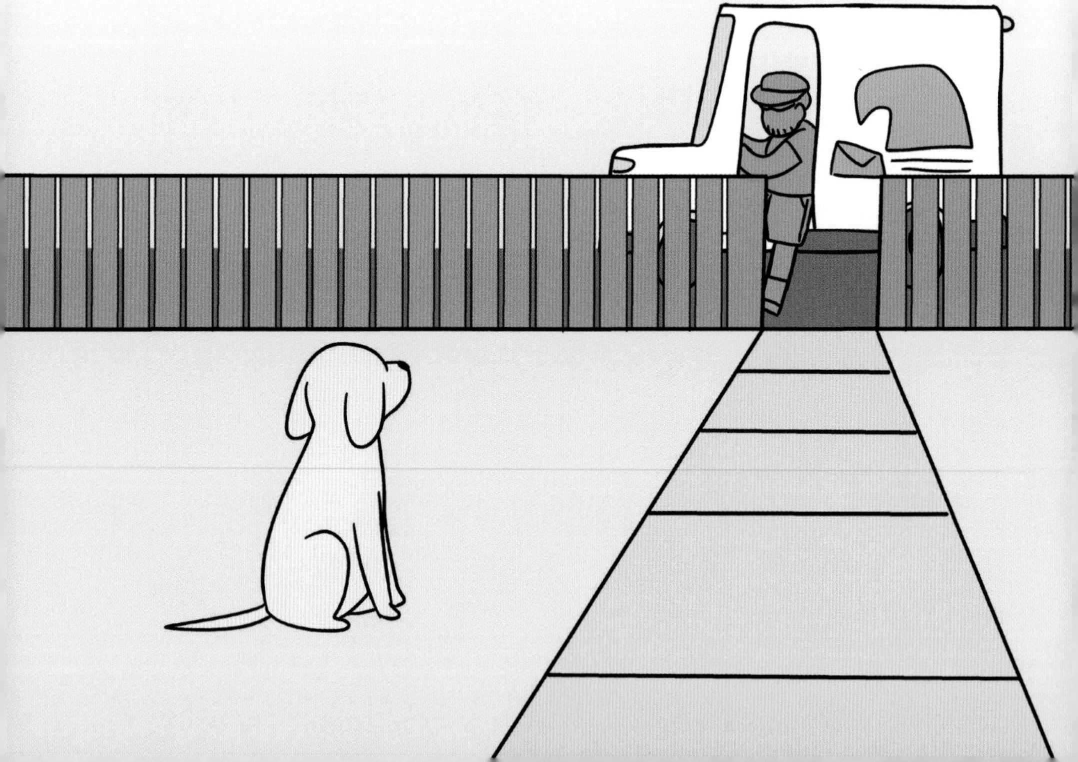

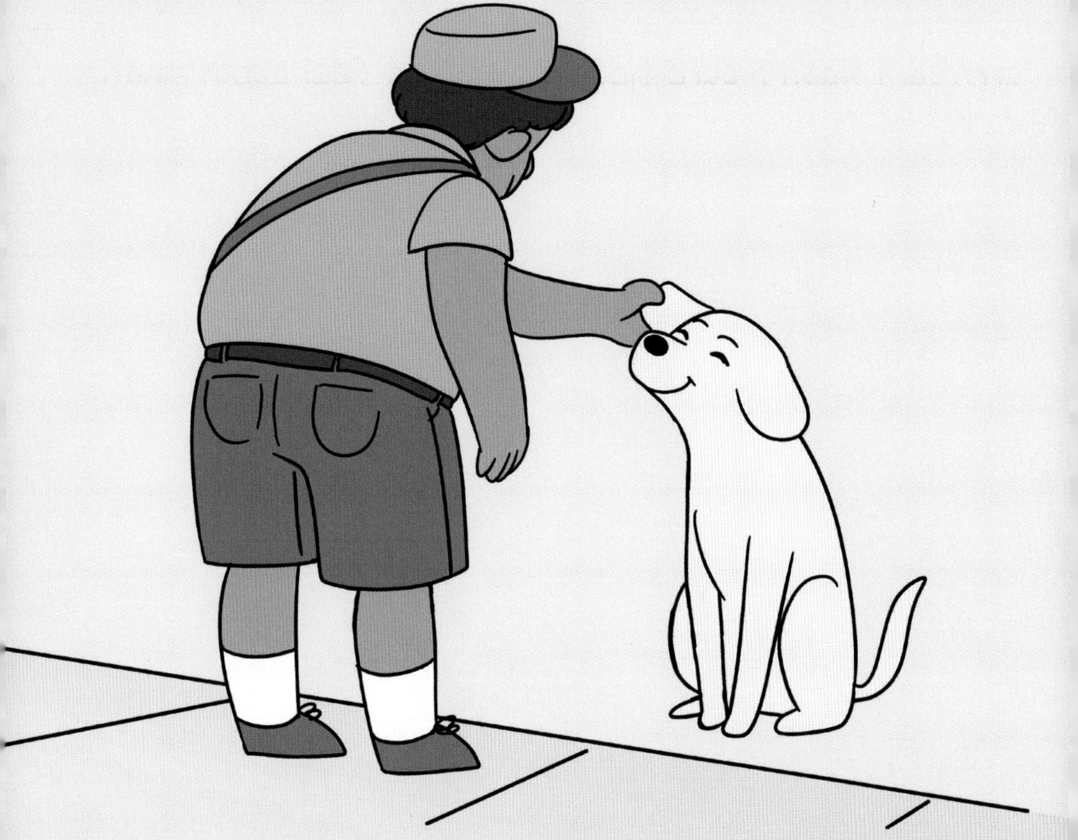

i was excited to see them slowly walk over. and rub my ear. before continuing on their way

the new mailman is back. and this time they had a treat for me. i accepted it and immediately ran inside. just to come back with my stuffed fren sebastian. so the new mailman could meet him too

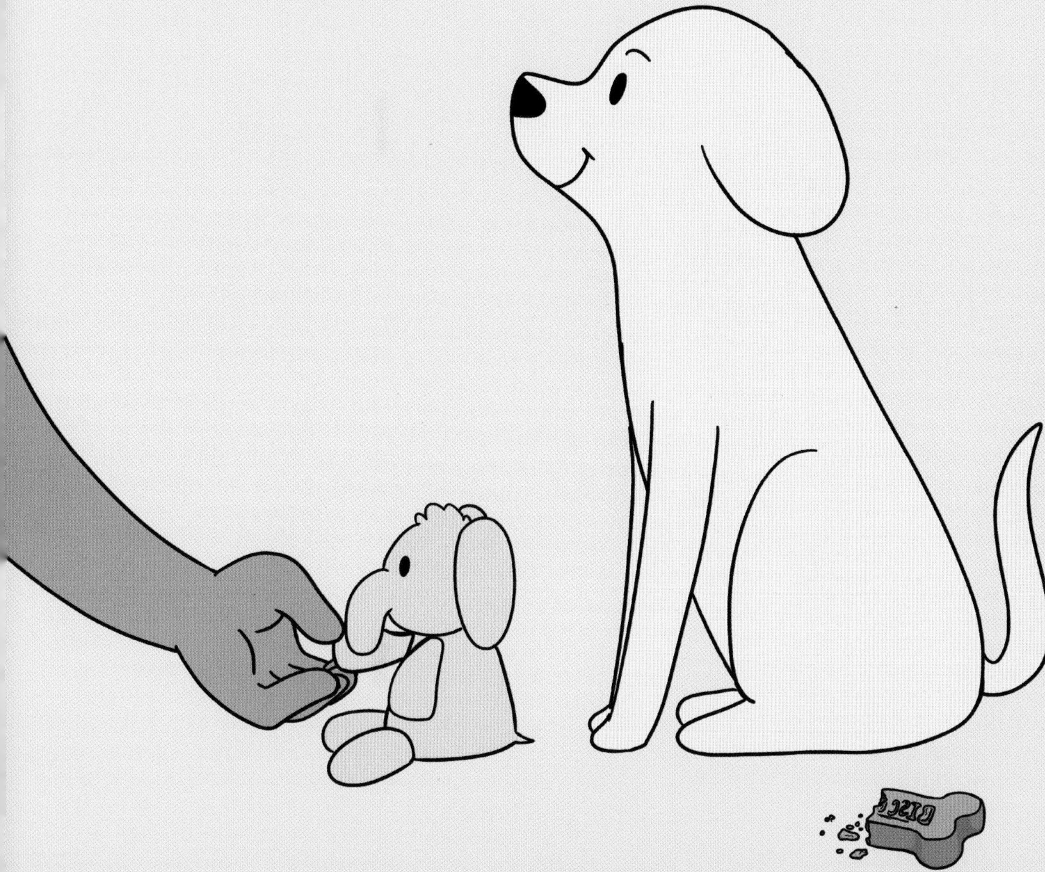

i heard the new mailman's van coming down the street.
so i decided to meet them before they even got out.

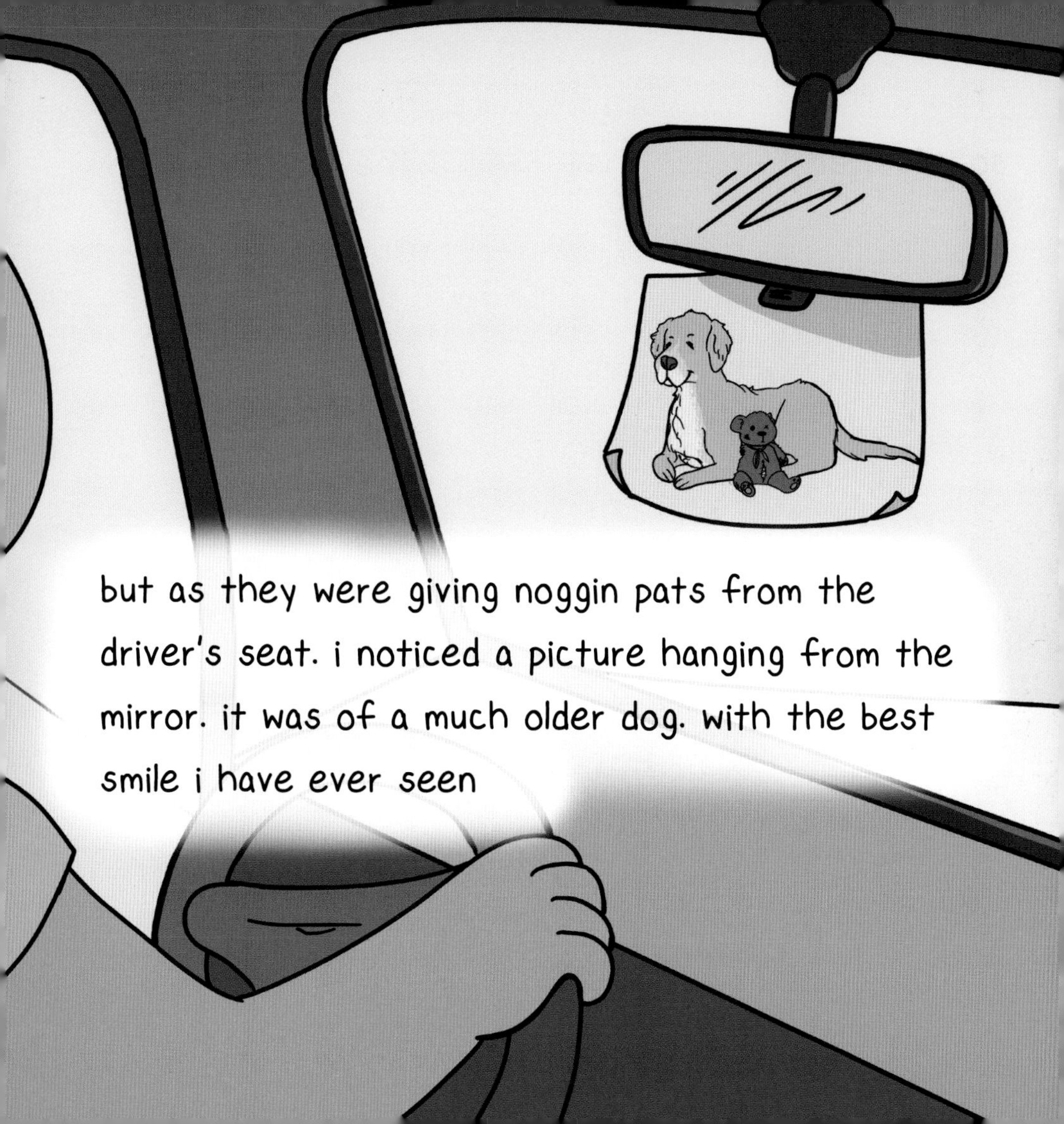

but as they were giving noggin pats from the driver's seat. i noticed a picture hanging from the mirror. it was of a much older dog. with the best smile i have ever seen

the new mailman is back today. and along with the
normal gifts. they knelt down to give me a toy. it
slightly resembled a bear. with several parts missing.
and the only smell coming from it was that of another
dog. when i looked back at the mailman. they sniffled a
few times. and wiped their face. the other stops can
wait. i think i'll lie in their lap for a while

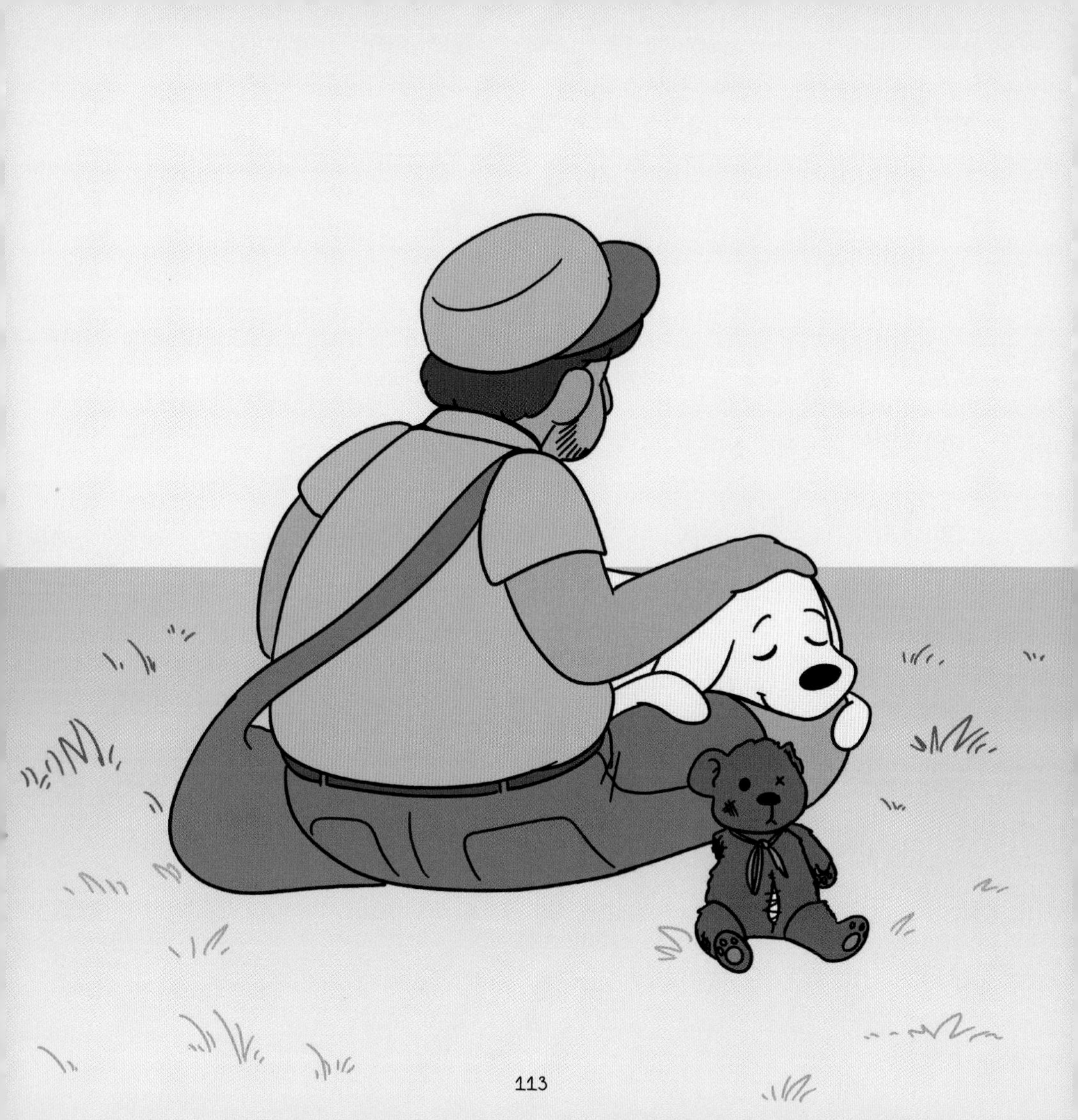

now. when the mailman stops by with the usual gifts.
i bring sebastian. and the bear. right to the window.
the mailman laughs every time. and we high five against
the glass

Acknowledgments

It'd be very off brand of me to start by thanking anyone other than Zoey and Sizzle, my two golden retrievers back home. I simply interpret their perfection. I'd also like to thank my family for their constant support; my agent, Kate McKean, for convincing my publisher to extend deadlines; my manager, Brian Canterbury; and the absolutely phenomenal illustrator of this book, Malory Pacheco, for bringing these stories to life. Finally, a huge thanks to my editor, Patty Rice, and everyone at Andrews McMeel for believing in the power of wholesome dog content.

About the Author

Matt Nelson is the creator behind two of the most treasured accounts on the Internet, Thoughts of Dog (@dog_feelings) and WeRateDogs (@dog_rates). Since launching the accounts in 2015 and 2017, Matt has built a community of more than 15 million followers combined. He currently resides in Los Angeles, CA. Find Matt on Twitter @dogfather.

Thoughts of Dog copyright © 2020 by Matt Nelson. All rights reserved. Printed in China. No part of this book may be used or reproduced in any manner whatsoever without written permission except in the case of reprints in the context of reviews.

Andrews McMeel Publishing
a division of Andrews McMeel Universal
1130 Walnut Street, Kansas City, Missouri 64106

www.andrewsmcmeel.com

Illustrations by Malory Pacheco

20 21 22 23 24 SDB 10 9 8 7 6 5 4 3 2 1

ISBN: 978-1-5248-5364-8

Library of Congress Control Number: 2020939609

Editor: Patty Rice
Art Director: Holly Swayne
Designer: Sierra S. Stanton
Production Editor: Margaret Daniels
Production Manager: Carol Coe

ATTENTION: SCHOOLS AND BUSINESSES
Andrews McMeel books are available at quantity discounts with
bulk purchase for educational, business, or sales promotional use.
For information, please e-mail the Andrews McMeel Publishing
Special Sales Department: specialsales@amuniversal.com.